CATERING TO CHARLESTON

Cherished Recipes

from a Premier Southern Caterer

Frances Ellison Hamby

HAMBY CATERING

Copyright © 2004 by Hamby Catering

First Edition

ISBN: 0-9747184-0-8

First Printing	7000 copies
Second Printing	7000 copies
Third Printing	7000 copies

Catering to Charleston
May be ordered by using the form in the back
of the book or address your request to:

HAMBY CATERING
925 St. Andrews Boulevard
Charleston, SC 29407
1-843-571-3103

WIMMER
COOKBOOKS

A CONSOLIDATED GRAPHICS COMPANY

800.548.2537 wimmerco.com

Caterer's Prayer

May we open our lives in relationship

with those who wait to be fed

with such bounty and joy.

"Give us this day, Lord, our daily bread,"

so that we may share with others the
"Bread of Life."

Elizabeth Bullock Godfrey

Special Thanks To:

Elizabeth "Lib" Godfrey for her encouragement and enthusiasm in the creation of this cookbook. Lib is a true Charlestonian, a graduate of the College of Charleston and a retiree from the Administrative Staff at the College. She has kindly allowed the use of her original poems and memories of growing up in Charleston.

Carol Simmons for her creative pen and ink drawings that have been placed throughout the book. Her work is primarily figurative using photo references and images drawn from her imagination and personal experiences. Her primary medium is oil. She also works with fiber, pastels, watercolors, charcoal and conte crayon. Her work is included in private collections nationwide and can be viewed locally at Gallery Chuma. She can be contacted at casimm@lycos.com.

First Federal for allowing the reproduction of artwork that originally appeared in *Famous Charleston Firsts*. All rights to the artwork are reserved and may not be reproduced in any form without the permission in writing from First Federal, publisher of *Famous Charleston Firsts*.

Daniel Quigly for his food photography used on the book cover.

Charleston Area Visitors Bureau for the photos used for the book cover. www. Charleston cvb.com. Their contact number is 1-800-868-8118.

Angie Basha for editorial and marketing assistance.

Diana Sproule for editing and technical expertise.

Catering to Charleston

Catering to Charleston is a tribute to our mother, Fran Hamby, the visionary founder of Hamby Catering. We are offering her favorite recipes so you can have the pleasure of preparing these fabulous dishes in your own kitchen.

For 25 years, Hamby Catering has grown from one woman's love of God, family and cooking into a thriving business representing the best in Southern cuisine.

The business began in Mother's kitchen when she and her friend, Syble, started planning her daughter's wedding reception. This first party was a huge success, and pretty soon several of Mother's friends were requesting help with their parties. As they say, the rest is history.

Catering to Charleston is a rare opportunity to glimpse into the rich culture of lavish entertaining that continues in Charleston today. Mother has prepared parties for local and national dignitaries. Past guests include President George Bush, Vice President Dan Quayle, Martha Stewart, Ted Turner, Jane Fonda, as well as several Governors and State Legislators and U.S. Congressmen.

Charleston's treasures are not only its extraordinary architecture, but also its exquisite cuisine. We passionately cherish both.

Rather than razing significant buildings and landmarks, we insist on restoration or finding adaptive uses in order to preserve them for tomorrow. Likewise, we go to great lengths to maintain the gracious dining and entertaining customs which are the spirit of Charleston hospitality.

Catering to Charleston honors the past generations who handed down a love of good food shared with good friends and equips the present and future generations to continue the legacy of spectacular Charleston entertaining with confidence bolstered by the surprisingly simple preparations and "Fran's Notes," which will make beginner cooks perform like accomplished professionals.

We proudly present **Catering to Charleston** in honor of two great ladies: Fran Hamby and Charleston, South Carolina!

Debra Hamby Bersinger

Steven T. Hamby

Frances Ellison Hamby

Best Cook, Caterer and Mother

It is our privilege to introduce our mother, Fran Hamby, the founder of Hamby Catering.

Mother's trademark, established early in her career, extends well beyond the expectations of elegant and delicious cuisine. It is one of grace that expresses her genuine love for people and joy in presenting them with unforgettable food experiences. She learned this from her family while growing up as the youngest of eleven children in upstate Williamston, South Carolina.

She first learned to cook on a wood-fired stove in the large farm kitchen, which was the center of activity. There her mother shared her recipes and family stories which usually involved food in some way.

Sunday dinner often brought as many as fifty friends and relatives, so Mother learned the skills of a caterer at a young age. Luckily, their farm yielded an abundance of home grown meats and vegetables, so there was always "a plenty."

Spiritual nourishment was not neglected, as Granddaddy would gather everyone for a session of Bible reading, reflection and prayer. Mother's grounding in food for the body and the soul fully prepared her for becoming Charleston's premier caterer.

Table of Contents

 LET'S HAVE A PARTY

On Meeting Street Where I Grew Up

The Crabapple tree leans against
the porch, holding tight it' buds
against the brisk March wind.
Pansies and Jonquils tease me into
the garden where I crunch an Oak
leaf path around Camellias, in
bloom. I wander out into the street
where I grew up.

Early Azalea blooms, protected
under Grand Oaks are beginning to
transform the neighborhood, and
Wisteria vines are climbing trees,
leaving a trail of grape-like clusters,
just as they do every year. Sixty
years ago, on this street at dusk,
Isaac pushed his cart, after a day's
catch with a "head-light" lit by a rag,
wicked in a can of kerosene nailed to

his cart. He chanted, as he strolled,
Lady git yo' dishpan, huh come de
swimp man swim-pee, swim-pee."
Another song comes to me. Beulah
balanced a large basket atop her head
and sang, "Veg-e-tub-bles, I got yo'
veg-e-tub-bles, fresh ok-ra, ta-ma-ta
and sweet pa-ta-ta."

We didn't think about the weight
they carried, only their music that
filled our street.

~ *Elizabeth Bullock Godfrey*

Let's Have A Party

Each entertaining occasion takes on its own personality. Birthdays, anniversaries, graduation, holidays and weekends are always great opportunities for celebrating. Develop a mental attitude that is geared toward being thankful, even for the small things, and share your joy with others through your hospitality. It is possible to entertain your family, friends and neighbors without wearing yourself to a frazzle. Your ultimate goal is for you and your guests to have a fantastic time. To do this, you must exceed your guests' expectations in terms of your theme, decorations, menu, presentation and service. Consistently exceeding your guests' expectations will earn for you a reputation as a fabulous and gracious hostess.

In planning your party, choose the set-up that will work best in your location and will provide the most contact and enjoyment for your guests. In general, your party will be set-up in one of three different formats: a cocktail reception, a dinner buffet or a seated meal.

A cocktail reception features a variety of hors d'oeuvres, served on platters and chafing dishes, and located in different areas of your party site. Your guests will mingle and interact with each other and have a bite whenever they choose. This format is ideal for functions where space and seating are limited.

The dinner buffet features a selection of entrées, side dishes and desserts, with your guests serving themselves from one central location. This format allows for a full meal to be served, while encouraging guests to mingle and converse. When setting up a buffet table for a large group, try to have doubles of each dish whenever possible. This allows guests to serve themselves from either side of the table.

A seated or served dinner features assigned seating for your guests, with servers bringing individual courses to each table. Generally, this is the most formal and intimate setting. It also requires the most space and labor.

The Ambiance

You must create an atmosphere that accentuates your theme. Let your imagination run wild. Lighting variation, linen choices, serving pieces, table configurations, floral selection and food centerpieces are all elements that can help you create your special ambiance. Fresh greenery, placed on your table around serving pieces, always adds a nice touch. If your theme is an elegant evening of cocktails and hors d' oeuvres in a historic home, then you should use your finest crystal, linens and silver. If you are hosting a backyard luau, then picnic tables with Hawaiian print linens, wood troughs and paper products are appropriate. Remember, if you don't have all the necessary equipment, you can probably rent it from a party rental store. Have anything you rent delivered the day before.

Planning Your Menu

Upon selecting your theme and party type, begin to focus on a menu that is compatible. With your budget in mind, make your menu selection broad enough so that there will be something for everyone. It is necessary to remember vegetarians as well as the meat-lovers. Choose your menu so that you have an ample selection of exciting and varied foods.

In planning your menu, consider the role of appetizers. These may be served buffet-style or passed by servers. Cocktail parties may feature a large selection of heavy or light hors d' oeuvres. If you are serving dinner with a rich and heavy entrée, choose lighter appetizers. Also, choose different foods for your appetizers than those chosen for the entrée.

No matter how large the meal, there is always room for dessert, the one food we, admittedly, eat purely for pleasure. Anything that finishes a meal can be called a dessert, from the grandest soufflé to a simple plate of cheese and fruit.

Executing Your Plan

The key to success is, do as much ahead of time as possible and have adequate help with all the work. Much of the labor can be done days in advance. Tables can be arranged, linens placed, utensils and serving pieces chosen. Save the day before and day of your party for the actual food preparation. Do as much food preparation as possible the day before the party. Also, remember, that you do not have to do everything yourself, order a special dish from a caterer or ask a friend to bring a dish.

When preparing a recipe, have all ingredients at room temperature unless otherwise instructed. Be sure to have the right ingredients and utensils ready with which to work. Read the recipe carefully before starting and measure correctly.

The final food preparations for your party are the trickiest. Timing is everything. Plan ahead and stick to your schedule. Remember that hot food is to be served hot and cold food cold. Also, remember that people eat with their eyes. All foods are more appetizing if they are attractive to the eye. Don't forget the garnishes. Hollowed shells of fruit and vegetables and flowers make serving platters and dinner plates come alive.

The first theater in America built especially for theatrical productions was constructed in Charleston in 1736, on Dock Street (now Queen). The current Dock Street Theatre, on the site of the old Planter's Hotel on Church Street, was reconstructed in 1936 from the plans of the original...and its opening that year saw the presentation of "The Recruiting Officer," which had been the first play staged in the original theatre 200 years earlier.

NEW YEAR'S DAY GOOD LUCK DINNER

Maple-Mustard Glazed Pork Roast, page 145

Oyster Pie, page 151

Hoppin' John, page 176

Maybell's Collard Greens, page 165

Blake's Favorite Macaroni and Cheese, page 171

Orange Glazed Carrots, page 165

Sister's Cornbread, page 84

Triple Chocolate Pound Cake, page 194

Tipsy Bread Pudding, page 197

Charlestonians have persevered through multiple disasters of fire, hurricanes and earthquakes. As the old saying goes, "Charleston - Hell or High water". It never hurts to start the New Year with a prayer of thanksgiving and plea for good luck. The Low Country has, traditionally, served collard greens, to ensure plenty of green-backs and Hoppin' John to provide extra change. Consider this simple and potent prayer for New Years day and every day throughout the year.

> *Dear Lord*
>
> *Please bring good luck to me*
> *The sea is so large*
> *My boat is so small*
> *Please be good to me*
> *Thank you. Amen.*

GOURMET CLUB ORIENTAL THEME DINNER

Egg Rolls, page 54
with
Sweet and Sour Sauce, page 54 and
Christen's Mustard Dipping Sauce, page 181

Shrimp-Fried Rice, page 158

Wok Cashew Chicken, page 140

Almond Bites, page 203

Tea

It is a great idea to start your own gourmet club. Consider forming a group of 8 to 10 friends that are interested in good food and friendship. The group may meet once a quarter and rotate the home and host. This is a wonderful format to try different ethnic cuisine or regional American favorites. The highlight will be friendships that will blossom while cooking in the kitchen together.

Friends that cook together,
stay together.

TRADD STREET COCKTAILS

Parmesan Squares, page 59

Spanakopita, page 62

Crab-Stuffed Mushrooms, page 32

Tomato Bruschetta, page 48

Spicy Cheese Straws, page 42

Cocktail Shrimp, page 38

Glazed Pork Tenderloin with Artichoke Relish, page 145

Finger Sandwiches

Salmon Mousse with Bremner Wafers, page 37

Hearts of Palm Dip with Pita Wedges, page 44

Asparagus Spears with Lemon Butter, page 162

Tray of Cheese Wedges and Fresh Fruit

Assortment of Mini-Sweets

Let's hope we are invited to this gracious Southern event. The table setting, flowers, music and crystal can all be a reflection of tranquility and charm. Bring out all of the candles and dim the lighting. Hors d' oeuvres passed on gleaming and shining silver trays exude a flair of elegance. Explore options for music - consider having someone perform on the harp, classical guitar or piano. This will help immensely in putting your party over the top for a 5-star rating.

EARLY TEE-TIME BREAKFAST

Fresh Squeezed Orange Juice

Sausage and Egg Casserole, page 90

Garlic Cheese Grits, page 87

Sliced Melon

Assorted Muffins, page 77

Golfers like to get an early start, so keep your menu and presentation simple and easy to prepare. Remember this is usually early and it is thoughtful to have something for that late riser that can be taken to go. A simple muffin and a hot cup of coffee will make that first shot long and straight.

GARDEN CLUB LUNCHEON BUFFET

Nutty Apple Salad, page 118

Chicken or Shrimp Supreme in Puff Pastry Shells, page 155

Asparagus Spears with Lemon Butter, page 165

Wild Rice with Dried Cranberries, page 178

Tomato Pie, page 165

Cream Cheese Biscuits, page 73

Strawberry-Raspberry Parfait, page 205

Garden clubs frequently meet in the members' homes. Show your table off to its best advantage with a large seasonal flower arrangement. Order extra flowers that you can arrange in small vases throughout the house. Remember, flowers always freshen up your décor. If seating is a problem, consider using bamboo trays. These are serviceable and add to the garden theme.

SULLIVAN'S ISLAND LUNCHEON

Shrimp Salad, page 116

Chicken Salad with Pineapple and Almonds, page 114

Curried Rice and Artichoke Salad, page 112

Marinated Green Beans or Asparagus, page 163

Fresh Mozzarella-Tomato Basil Salad, page 110

Croissants with Sweet Butter

Crème Caramel, page 196

What could be finer than this delicious cold lunch served in a beach house setting on a hot summer day? Pastel Fiesta Ware, plaid summer linens and large pitchers of minted iced tea will provide a spirited, eye-appealing greeting for your guests. Accent your table presentation with fresh summer flowers, casually arranged in your favorite beach-ware vase.

The first rice to be planted in America was grown in Charleston almost as soon as the colony was settled. A sea captain named Thurber brought a peck of rice seed from Madagascar Island to one of the leading settlers, Dr. Henry Woodward of Charleston, who found that the grain grew well here. By 1690 rice was being exported, and by 1700 "there were not enough ships in the harbor to export (all the rice)," according to the Collector of Customs. Carolina Long Grain Rice became the criteria by which rice was judged, and generated a plantation society whose wealth, educaiton, and political power was unequalled in the world.

LET'S HAVE A PARTY

SUNDAY BRUNCH BUFFET

Hamby's Buttermilk Biscuits Filled with Ham, page 73

Vegetable Frittata, page 94

Breakfast Shrimp with Grits, page 88

Golden Hash Brown Casserole, page 93

Sliced Tomatoes

Ambrosia Salad, page 117

Yogurt Fruit Scones, page 83, Banana-Nut Bread, page 82,
and Blueberry Muffins, page 79

Butter, Cream Cheese and Assorted Jams

Spicy Cheese Straws, page 42

Sunday brunches often follow some type of very late Saturday evening celebration. Therefore, a late starting time is appropriate. Some guests may arrive a little early and enjoy a Bloody Mary or Mimosa as an eye-opener. Garnishes that make bars memorable are celery stalks, fresh cut lime and orange slices, pickled okra, dilly beans, hot peppers, and don't forget that old time favorite, Tabasco sauce.

LET'S HAVE A PARTY

SUNDAY EVENING YOUTH GROUP

Chicken Tex-Mex Barbecue, page 133

Potato Chips or Sticks

Marinated Coleslaw, page 109

Crisp Carrot and Celery Sticks

Olives, Pickles

Over-Sized Chocolate Chip Cookies, page 201

Fran's Orange Muffins, page 80

Beverage

Our family has a long tradition of Sunday evening church attendance. The only difference now is that we cook rather than eat. Casual food and old-fashioned games such as volleyball, soccer, kick ball and softball are still a winning combination.

> *"Train up a child in the*
> *way he should go:*
> *and when he is old,*
> *he will not depart from it."*
>
> *Proverbs 22:6*

LET'S HAVE A PARTY

LOW COUNTRY FALL GET-TOGETHER

Boiled Peanuts, page 182

Spicy Cheese Straws, page 42

Steamed Oysters with Cocktail Sauce

Frogmore Stew, page 157

Pulled Pork BBQ with Sliced White Bread, page 144

Charleston Red Rice, page 173

Squash Casserole, page 167

Marinated Coleslaw, page 109

Sister's Corn Bread, page 84

Lib's Apple Crisp, page 186

When the leaves start changing in color and the air becomes crisp, head outside for fun and food. Oysters begin to be harvested more abundantly in the Low Country beginning in the month of October. These local oysters are favorites due to their reputation as a saltier treat. Burlap bags, wood crates, wood boxes, bales of hay, and pumpkins make great festive decorations.

THANKSGIVING FEAST

Roast Turkey, page 146 and Giblet Gravy, page 147

Cornbread Dressing, page 147

Cranberry-Orange Relish, page 180

Duchess Potatoes, page 166

Artichoke Bottoms Stuffed with Spinach, page 162

Green Beans with Sautéed Slivered Almonds, page 163

Orange Glazed Carrots, page 165

Sweet Potato Soufflé, page 167

Holiday Cranberry Salad, page 119

Crusty French Rolls with Butter

Chocolate Pecan Pie, page 198

Rachel's Favorite Pumpkin Cake Roll, page 206

Thanksgiving traditionally is a time for family. Extend your concept to include friends and neighbors. Imagine your home with a large bannistered front porch and a surrounding picket fence as the setting for this special autumn gathering. Invite everyone to come early, so as not to miss the fun of preparations for the upcoming feast. Of course, encourage everyone to participate. Let young children make the old-fashioned pinecone turkey decorations for the children's table.

Left over construction paper can be used to make Indian headbands and pilgrim hats. While the turkey is baking, let the older youth and adults break out games such as Scrabble, Cranium and Trivial Pursuit, which will stimulate lots of fun and laughter.

Living well begins at your home.

HAMBY'S CHRISTMAS GET-TOGETHER

Cocktail Shrimp, page 38

Parmesan Squares, page 59

Beef Tenderloin Stuffed with Lobster Tails, page 131

Glazed Ham, page 143

Blake's Favorite Macaroni and Cheese, page 171

Holiday Cranberry Salad, page 119

Oven-Roasted Vegetables, page 169

Tangy Green Beans with Pimiento, page 164

Sweet Potato Soufflé, page 167

Ambrosia Salad, page 117

Aunt Julie's White Fruit Cake, page 191

Dixie Pecan Pie, page 199

Let Christmas be a season of family entertainment and create your own traditions for generations. Focus your traditions on quality and style. This is always a busy season, so plan in advance. This menu includes several items that can be made in advance. Decorate your home with live poinsettias and large amounts of greenery. The scent of fresh greenery will long be remembered. The food will be simply brilliant and the spirit of the season will shine through. The main thought to leave with you is:

Relax and Enjoy Yourself

SCARLETT'S WEDDING RECEPTION

Butlered Hors D'oeuvres*

*Country Ham on Sweet Potato Biscuits, page 74

*Spicy Shrimp Wrapped in Snow Peas, page 40

*Crab-Stuffed Mushrooms, page 32

*Linda's Fried Oysters, page 149
with Rémoulade Sauce, page 180

Spicy Cheese Straws, page 42

Fresh Fruit and Cheese Display with Chocolate Fondue

Raw and Marinated Vegetable Display

Dad's Pimiento Cheese Spread, page 42

Finger Sandwiches

Asparagus Spears with Lemon Butter, page 162

Stuffed Cherry Tomatoes, page 49

Shrimp and Grits Station

Breakfast Shrimp with Grits, page 88

Crab Cake Station with Chef

Crab Cakes Imperial, page 148

Lemon Dill Sauce, page 179 and Fresh Tomato Salsa, page 181

Okra and Tomato Pilaf, page 176

Carving Station with Chef

Filet of Beef Tenderloin, page 130

Rolls, Breads and Condiments

Roast Turkey, page 146

Cranberry-Orange Relish, page 180

Breads

Seafood Extravaganza on Ice

Chilled Shrimp with Cocktail Sauce

Low Country Blue Crab Fingers, page 148
with Christen's Mustard Sauce, page 181

Poached Scallops with Horseradish and Lime Sauce, page 152

Osetra Caviar Served with Toast Points, Cream Cheese, Grated Egg Yolks &
Chopped Egg Whites, Red Onion and Capers

Wedding Cake

Coffee Station

SCARLETT'S WEDDING

Hamby Catering is perhaps most famous for it spectacular wedding receptions and rehearsal dinners. This is where the business began and it is still true that Hamby loves their brides. It is our belief that every bride and groom deserves the best and it is our utmost desire to provide just that.

Specialty stations have become anticipated themes of Low Country receptions. These stations have a chef cooking and serving the food individually for each guest. This experience can include shrimp and grits with tasso gravy, grilled quail with Raspberry sauce, baby lamb chops with tzatziki sauce and stir-fry chicken and beef. Our clients frequently request a sushi station. These individual stations add just the right touch of sophistication and style.

The main tables usually include lavish fruit and flower displays. Numerous chafing dishes contain foods like hot artichoke dip with a tray of melba rounds alongside, hot spinach dip, bacon-wrapped scallops and crab mornay. There are magnificent artfully displayed trays of finger sandwiches, cherry stuffed tomatoes and baked mushroom squares.

Southern receptions often feature a seafood extravaganza displayed on ice. Watch the guests' faces from near and far light up with delight as they gaze at the 5-foot tall ice sculpture surrounded by cascading shrimp, scallops, oysters and mussels. Hot mini crab cakes being served by a chef at an adjacent station can create a rush.

Of course, there can never be too many choices. The carving station with tenderloin of beef, pork tenderloin and smoked turkey are beckoning like a siren with the fragrant aroma. Picture a large beef steamship round being carved by a formally attired chef and served with hot rolls accompanied by horseradish, mustard and mayonnaise sauces. The ham biscuits are going too like hot cakes.

Rehearsal dinners also have many options and may be more casual events. Pig roasts, oyster roasts and frogmore stew functions can start the festivities off right.

Charleston is now one of the most desirable locations and destinations for weddings. These pre-wedding events now often include friends and out of town guests.

My brother, Steve, is involved greatly in the day-to-day operations of our catering business. When asked what his best suggestion would be regarding wedding receptions, his reply is "just call the professional." As a totally biased sister, I say "just call Hamby Catering."

 **APPETIZERS**
AND
BEVERAGES

Persistence and Grace

Hurricanes churn Atlantic waters
forcing tides to rise and giant waves
to hammer Charleston's Battery Wall
flooding much of the city. Brutal winds
batter hundred-year old oaks, ripping away
porches and chimney pots and peeling back

tin roofs, quickly, like chewing gum
wrappers. Tornadoes follow, swooping
down, shattering window panes, pulling
away Corinthian columns and lifting roof
trusses and slate shingles, tossing them to
the ground, leaving a heap of rubbish.

Eighteenth and nineteenth century buildings,
built fortress-like, with walls of interlocking
brick courses, some have crumbled, others
beaten up, yet standing, bearing scars.
Cannon balls have grazed them, earthquakes
cracked and dazed them but walls are
patched with stucco hiding scars, hand-scored to
look like stone,transformed and reinforced with
rods, decorated with lion heads and crosses.
And through it all, a spirit of persistence and
grace breathes it's presence in this place.

~ *Elizabeth Bullock Godfrey*

REFLECTIONS

A Charlestonian by birth, my life was influenced by a culture that was known as "...the only Chinese city in America where people, still, eat rice and worship their ancestors". Yes, rice was served at mid-day dinner almost every day and, yes, we had a strong identity with our grandparents and a host of aunts, uncles, and cousins, who lived close by. My three brothers and I represented the fourth generation, who followed the tradition of working in our mother's family's bake shop, BECKROGE'S BAKERY. The bakery was founded by our great-grandfather, with the assistance of his Pastor and mentor, Louis Mueller, of St. Matthew's Lutheran Church. He came to Charleston from Germany when he was eleven.

~ *Elizabeth Bullock Godfrey*

John's Island Crab Dip

MAKES 4 CUPS

1 pound backfin crabmeat, well drained

2 teaspoons horseradish

⅓ cup small capers, drained

¾ teaspoon lemon zest

Dash of Tabasco sauce

2 cups mayonnaise

¾ cup shredded sharp Cheddar cheese

Assorted crackers

Combine crabmeat, horseradish, capers, zest, Tabasco and mayonnaise. Spread mixture into a greased 1 quart casserole dish. Sprinkle cheese on top. Bake at 350 degrees until bubbly. Serve hot with crackers.

FRAN'S NOTE

Lump crabmeat is larger chunks than backfin crabmeat. Lump crabmeat is preferable for some recipes, but I find backfin crabmeat works well in most recipes. It is important to pick over crabmeat to remove any residual shell pieces.

Tidewater Cold Crab Spread

MAKES 3½ CUPS

3 (8-ounce) packages cream cheese, softened

3 tablespoons Worcestershire sauce

2 tablespoons lemon juice

5 tablespoons mayonnaise

3 small green onions, white parts minced

1 (12-ounce) bottle chili sauce

1 pound fresh crabmeat

Chopped parsley for garnish

Assorted crackers

Cream together cream cheese, Worcestershire sauce, juice, mayonnaise and onions. Spread over bottom of 13x9x2 inch baking dish. Pour on chili sauce and top with crabmeat. Sprinkle with parsley and serve with crackers.

Crabmeat Mousse

MAKES 25 SERVINGS

1   (¼-ounce) envelope unflavored gelatin

¼   cup cold water

½   cup boiling water

½   cup mayonnaise

2   tablespoons finely snipped fresh chives or ½ teaspoon dried

2   tablespoons finely chopped fresh dill

1   tablespoon minced onion

1   tablespoon fresh lemon juice

Dash of Tabasco sauce

¼   teaspoon paprika

1   teaspoon salt

2   cups flaked lump crabmeat, picked for shells

1   cup heavy cream, whipped

Fresh dill sprigs for garnish

Bremner wafers

Soften the gelatin in the cold water in a large mixing bowl for 3 minutes. Whisk in the boiling water until the gelatin dissolves. Cool to room temperature. Stir in mayonnaise, chives, dill, onions, juice, Tabasco, paprika and salt. Whisk until well blended. Fold in crabmeat and whipped cream. Pour mixture into a well-greased 5 cup mold and refrigerate overnight. Unmold onto a platter, garnish with dill sprigs and serve with Bremner wafers.

Crab-Stuffed Mushrooms

MAKES 24 MUSHROOMS

24 large white button mushrooms, rinsed in cold water and patted dry

8 tablespoons butter, melted

1 tablespoon all-purpose flour

½ teaspoon salt

¼ teaspoon celery salt

Dash of cayenne pepper

½ cup half-and-half

2 tablespoons mushroom stems, chopped

1 tablespoon chopped parsley

1 tablespoon sherry

1 pound crabmeat, shell and cartilage removed

3 tablespoons grated Parmesan cheese

¼ teaspoon paprika

Remove mushroom stems and chop. Reserve caps. Blend butter, flour, salt, celery salt, and cayenne in a saucepan. Gradually add half-and-half. Cook, stirring constantly, until thick and smooth. Add chopped mushrooms, parsley and sherry and mix well. Fold in crabmeat. Stuff mushroom caps with crabmeat mixture. Sprinkle with cheese and paprika. Place on a well-greased 15x10x1 inch baking sheet. Bake at 350 degrees 15 to 20 minutes or until lightly brown.

The Colonies' first independent flag was designed in 1775 by Colonel William Moultrie, then commanding the state militia units that occupied Fort Johnson, the harbor's major defense bastion. The blue flag was decorated with a white crescent, in honor of the crescents which decorated the hats of the militia. That flag was the basis for South Carolina's present state flag; the palmetto tree was added by the legislature January 28, 1861, in honor of the successful defeat of the British at the palmetto-log fort later to be named for Moultrie.

Party Artichoke and Crab Dip

1 large bell pepper, chopped

1 tablespoon vegetable oil

2 (14-ounce) cans artichoke hearts, drained and finely chopped

2 cups mayonnaise

½ cup chopped green onions

1 cup freshly grated Parmesan cheese

1½ teaspoons lemon juice

4 teaspoons Worcestershire sauce

½ cup chopped pimiento, drained

3 jalapeño peppers, chopped

1 teaspoon celery salt

1 pound backfin crabmeat

⅓ cup slivered almonds

Pita chips

Sauté peppers in oil. Add artichokes, mayonnaise, onions, Parmesan cheese, juice, Worcestershire sauce, pimientos, jalapeño peppers and celery salt. Fold in crabmeat. Pour mixture into a 2 quart casserole dish. Top with almonds and bake at 375 degrees 20 minutes or until bubbly. Serve with pita chips.

Pita Chips

MAKES 16 TO 20 SERVINGS

8 large pita breads

8 tablespoons butter, softened

Salt to taste

Separate each pita bread into 2 circles. Spread butter over pita halves and sprinkle lightly with salt. Cut into ⅛ inch pieces. Bake at 350 degrees 8 to 12 minutes. May be made 1 day in advance. Serve rough side up.

Crabmeat Mornay

MAKES ABOUT 50 APPETIZERS

8	tablespoons butter	½	teaspoon salt
1	small bunch green onions, chopped	1	pint half-and-half
⅓	cup parsley, finely chopped	1	pound backfin crabmeat
2	tablespoons all-purpose flour	½	pound grated Swiss cheese
¼	teaspoon cayenne pepper	1	tablespoon sherry
			Melba rounds or pastry shells

Melt butter in heavy saucepan. Sauté onions and parsley. Add flour, cayenne and salt. Cook 4 minutes. Blend in half-and-half and cook until slightly thickened. Gently fold in crabmeat, cheese and sherry. Heat thoroughly, but do not boil. Serve in a chafing dish with Melba rounds or in miniature pastry shells.

Oysters on the Half Shell with Pernod Dipping Sauce

MAKES 8 SERVINGS

½	cup champagne vinegar or white wine vinegar	1	tablespoon minced sweet red pepper
⅓	cup dry white wine		Salt and pepper to taste
4	teaspoons Pernod		Crushed ice
4	teaspoons minced green onion	24	fresh oysters, top shell removed

Combine vinegar, wine, Pernod, onions and peppers in medium bowl. Season with salt and pepper. (Sauce may be prepared 2 hours ahead. Cover and let stand at room temperature.) Cover serving platter with crushed ice. Top with oysters. Place dipping sauce in center of platter. Serve immediately.

Oysters Rockefeller

MAKES 24 SERVINGS

Rock salt

24 oysters on the half shell

4 tablespoons butter

3 tablespoons sliced green onion

3 tablespoons minced parsley

½ cup bread crumbs

1½ cups fresh spinach, rinsed, drained and chopped

2 tablespoons Pernod or to taste

1 teaspoon celery salt

2 teaspoons lemon juice

¼ teaspoon cayenne

24 (1 inch) size bacon pieces, uncooked

½ cup Parmesan cheese

Preheat oven to 425 degrees. Fill six 8 inch pie pans with rock salt. Place oysters in shell on rock salt. Heat butter in heavy skillet until foaming. Sauté onions until soft. Stir in parsley, bread crumbs, spinach, Pernod, celery powder, juice and cayenne. Mix thoroughly. Spoon a teaspoon of spinach mixture onto oysters, distributing evenly. Top each oyster with bacon piece. Place pans in oven and bake 8 to 10 minutes or until bacon is crisp. Remove from oven and sprinkle with Parmesan cheese. Serve directly from pie pan.

FRAN'S NOTE

To serve canapés without shells or forks, remove oysters from shells and place on crisp toast rounds or in individual ovenproof crocks. Proceed as directed above.

Hearts of Palm Wrapped with Smoked Salmon

MAKES 36 SERVINGS

Raspberry Dressing

2	tablespoons raspberry vinegar	½	teaspoon salt
3	teaspoons lemon juice	½	cup olive oil
1	tablespoon Dijon mustard		

Salmon

1	(16-ounce) can hearts of palm, drained	½	pound smoked salmon, cut into thin strips

Raspberry Dressing

Combine vinegar, juice, mustard, salt and oil in jar. Seal tightly, shake well and refrigerate.

Salmon

Cut hearts of palm crosswise into thirds. Wrap a salmon strip around each piece. Arrange in a serving dish in spoke wheel fashion. Cover and refrigerate for several hours or overnight. Just before serving, top with a generous amount of raspberry dressing.

Salmon Mousse

MAKES 6 CUPS

2 (¼-ounce) enveloped unflavored gelatin

⅓ cup cold water

½ cup boiling water

¾ cup mayonnaise

2 tablespoons lemon juice

1½ tablespoons grated onion

2 teaspoons Tabasco sauce or to taste

⅓ teaspoon paprika

1 teaspoon salt

2 teaspoons dried dill or to taste

1 (14¾-ounce) can Red Sockeye Salmon, flaked

1½ cups heavy cream, whipped

Pumpernickel bread or toast points

Soften the gelatin in cold water in a mixing bowl. Whisk in boiling water until gelatin dissolves. Cool. Add mayonnaise, juice, onions, Tabasco, paprika, salt and dill. Mix well and refrigerate until it resembles unbeaten egg whites. Add salmon. Fold in whipped cream. Pour into a slightly greased fish mold. Refrigerate until set. Serve with toast points or pumpernickel bread slices.

Pickled Shrimp

MAKES 10 SERVINGS

1¼ cups vegetable oil

¾ cup white vinegar

1½ teaspoons salt

1 teaspoon celery salt

2 tablespoons capers, with juice

1 tablespoon sugar or to taste

2 pounds shelled shrimp, cooked

1 large bell pepper, seeded and sliced into rings

3 medium onions, thinly sliced

Combine oil, vinegar, salt, celery salt, capers and sugar to make a marinade. Refrigerate. Layer shrimp, peppers and onions in a shallow serving dish. Pour the marinade over top. Cover and refrigerate for 24 hours, turning shrimp occasionally. May store in refrigerator for several days.

Cocktail Shrimp

MAKES 8 SERVINGS

Cocktail Sauce

1	cup ketchup	1	tablespoon fresh lemon juice
1	tablespoon prepared horseradish		

Shrimp

8	cups water	**Salt to taste**
2	teaspoons salt	**Fresh lemon juice**
2	pounds raw, peeled and deveined shrimp	

Cocktail Sauce

Whisk ketchup, horseradish and juice in small bowl until well blended. Cover and refrigerate. Makes 1⅛ cups.

Shrimp

Bring salted water to boil. Add shrimp, return to boil then simmer about 3 minutes. Do not overcook. Drain shrimp and plunge into ice water to stop the cooking. When cold, remove shrimp and season with salt and lemon juice. Serve with cocktail sauce.

FRAN'S NOTE

Raw shrimp turn pink and firm when done. It takes
about 3 minutes to boil 1 pound of medium-sized shrimp.

FRAN'S NOTE

Allow approximately 2 to 3 ounces of shrimp per person or 15 to 20 pounds for 100. You want to have a decent amount. I would rather not serve them at all if there are not enough to go around. There are several attractive ways to display and serve shrimp. One of my favorite ways consists of putting crushed ice in a plastic bag and place in bottom of a large Lucite shell. Cover with lettuce, mound shrimp on top and decorate with lemon slices. Of course, they look beautiful in a silver punch bowl or large seashell. Next to the shrimp, place a medium seashell filled with cocktail sauce and a small spoon. By placing a small spoon in the cocktail sauce, you encourage the guests to put some on their plates, take a few shrimp and hopefully, walk away. This allows more people to have access to the shrimp and also, prevents dipping more than once. Place another shell or plate nearby for discarded toothpicks.

Mrs. Patrick's Shrimp Paste

MAKES 6 SERVINGS

1 pound medium sized shrimp, cooked, peeled and deveined	Juice of half a lemon
½ teaspoon salt or to taste	¼ teaspoon Tabasco sauce
¼ teaspoon celery seeds	¼ cup of mayonnaise or more to bind mixture
¼ teaspoon minced onion	Assorted mild crackers

In a food processor, coarsely chop shrimp. Combine together shrimp, salt, celery seeds, onions, juice and Tabasco. Add mayonnaise and stir until mixture holds together. Cover and refrigerate. Serve with mild crackers.

FRAN'S NOTE

This recipe may be used as a filling for shrimp sandwiches.

Spicy Shrimp Wrapped in Snow Peas

MAKES 20 WRAPS

20 uncooked large shrimp, peeled and deveined

1 tablespoon minced fresh ginger

2 teaspoons vegetable oil

1 large garlic clove, pressed

½ teaspoon Chinese 5-spice powder

20 large snow peas, trimmed and stringed

1 teaspoon oriental sesame oil

½ teaspoon sesame seeds, toasted

2 tablespoons soy sauce

20 small wooden skewers or toothpicks

Combine shrimp, ginger, oil, garlic and Chinese powder in medium bowl and toss until coated. Cover and refrigerate at least 1 hour or up to 4 hours. Cook peas in boiling salted water for 45 seconds or just until crisp-tender. Drain and rinse in cold water. Drain and pat dry. Transfer peas to a bowl. Drizzle with sesame oil and sesame seeds and toss until coated. Set aside. Heat a large nonstick skillet over medium-high heat. Sauté shrimp mixture for 3 minutes. Add soy sauce. Cook and stir for 1 minute until shrimp are just opaque in center and liquid evaporates. Remove to a plate and cool completely. Wrap 1 snow pea lengthwise around each shrimp from head to tail. Secure with skewers. Cover and refrigerate. May be prepared 6 hours in advance. Serve chilled or at room temperature.

Chutney Cheese Ball

MAKES 20 SERVINGS

4   (3-ounce) packages cream cheese, softened

6   green onions, sliced

½   cup raisins

8   slices bacon, cooked and crumbled

2   tablespoons sour cream

1   teaspoon curry powder

⅓   cup peanuts, chopped

1   (12-ounce) jar mango chutney

Flaked coconut

Combine cream cheese, onions, raisins, bacon, sour cream, curry, peanuts and half of the chutney. Form mixture into a ball on waxed paper. Place on serving platter and pour remaining chutney over ball. Sprinkle with coconut.

FRAN'S TIP

Guideline for serving guests.

Cheese and crackers: For 100 servings, you will need 5 pounds of assorted cheeses and 3 to 4 pounds of crackers. Muenster and Cheddar cheese are good with fruit. Select crackers that will not mask the flavor of the cheese. Choose crackers that are not highly flavored with onion, garlic and spices.

Nuts: Allow 1 pound per 25 guests. Put the expensive mixed nuts on the cake table with the mints. Place napkin-lined baskets of cocktail peanuts near the bar with pretzels and deviled eggs.

Mints: Allow 2 or 3 per person.
One 8-ounce box serves approximately 40 guests.

Dad's Pimiento Cheese Spread

MAKES 3 CUPS

12 ounces mild Cheddar cheese

1 (4-ounce) jar pimiento, finely chopped and well drained

½ teaspoon minced garlic

1 teaspoon horseradish

1 tablespoon burgundy wine

1 teaspoon Durkee's Famous Sauce

1 teaspoon Worcestershire sauce

¼ teaspoon coarse ground black pepper or to taste

3 tablespoons Miracle Whip

3 tablespoons mayonnaise

Combine cheese, pimiento, garlic, horseradish, wine, Durkee's sauce, Worcestershire sauce, pepper, Miracle Whip and mayonnaise. Serve with assorted crackers.

Spicy Cheese Straws

MAKES APPROXIMATELY 100 STRAWS OR MORE

2 (8-ounce) packages shredded sharp Cheddar cheese

16 tablespoons margarine, softened

2⅓ cups all-purpose flour

¼ teaspoon salt

1 teaspoon baking powder

½ teaspoon cayenne pepper

Grate cheese in a food processor. Beat margarine and cheese with an electric mixer until very smooth. Blend in flour, salt, baking powder and cayenne. Use a cookie press with a star-shaped filler tip. Shoot dough onto baking sheet into 3 inch finger-length strips. Bake at 300 to 325 degrees 15 to 20 minutes. Do not overcook.

Brie with Amaretto and Walnuts

1   (10-ounce) round Brie cheese
½   cup packed brown sugar
¼   cup Amaretto liqueur

½   cup coarsely chopped walnuts
Assorted crackers, bread and
    apple slices

Preheat oven to 400 degrees. Remove the top rind of Brie. Place in a shallow baking dish. Mix brown sugar, Amaretto and walnuts. Spread over top of cheese. Bake 8 to 10 minutes or until cheese melts. Keep warm and serve with assorted crackers, bread and apple slices.

Low Country Artichoke Dip

MAKES 3 CUPS

1   (14-ounce) can of artichoke
    hearts, drained and squeezed
    dry
1   cup mayonnaise
1   cup grated Parmesan cheese

¼   teaspoon seasoning salt
¼   teaspoon garlic powder
½   cup canned chopped green
    chilies (optional)
Melba rounds

Chop artichokes. Combine artichokes with mayonnaise, Parmesan cheese, seasoning salt, garlic powder and green chilies. Place mixture in a 1 quart casserole dish. Bake at 350 degrees 20 minutes. Serve with Melba rounds.

Deb's Hot Artichoke Dip

MAKES 3 CUPS

2 (14-ounce) cans of artichoke hearts, drained and chopped

1 (6-ounce) package crumbled blue cheese

4 tablespoons butter, melted

Melba rounds or shredded wheat crackers

Combine artichokes, blue cheese and butter. Pour into an 8-inch pie pan. Bake at 350 degrees 20 minutes. Serve hot with Melba rounds or shredded wheat crackers. If you double or triple recipe, use ¼ less butter. Triple the recipe to fill a 2 quart chafing dish.

Hearts of Palm Dip

MAKES 3 CUPS

1 (14-ounce) can hearts of palm, drained and chopped

1 cup mayonnaise

¼ cup sour cream

1 cup shredded mozzarella cheese

½ cup grated Parmesan cheese

2 tablespoons sliced green onions

¼ teaspoon garlic salt

¼ teaspoon cayenne pepper

Shredded wheat crackers or toast points

Combine hearts of palm, mayonnaise, sour cream, cheeses, onions, garlic salt and cayenne and mix well. Spread mixture into a 9 inch pie plate. Bake at 350 degrees 20 minutes. Serve hot with shredded wheat crackers or toast points.

Chafing Dish Broccoli

MAKES 4 CUPS

2 (10-ounce) packages frozen chopped broccoli, thawed

1 medium onion, chopped

2 tablespoons butter, melted

1 (10¾-ounce) can cream of mushroom soup

Dash of cayenne pepper

2 rolls pasteurized garlic cheese spread

1 (4-ounce) jar sliced mushrooms, drained

¾ cup slivered almonds

Crackers or corn chip scoops

Cook broccoli and drain. Sauté onions in butter. Add soup, cayenne and cheese. Cook and stir over low heat until cheese melts. Add broccoli and cook 1 minute. Stir in mushrooms and almonds. Serve hot with crackers or scoops.

FRAN'S NOTE

May use well-squeezed frozen spinach in place of broccoli.

Blue Ribbon Children

Back in 1938, I was a first-grader. At that time there was a big push to have children inoculated with the small pox vaccine. The children who did so were rewarded by having their picture taken as a group. When the "Charleston Evening Post" was delivered with that picture, I remember that feeling of pride and distinction as I spread it open on the bed and thought, "That's Me."

~ Elizabeth Bullock Godfrey

Black-Eyed Pea Dip

MAKES 16 TO 20 SERVINGS

4   (16-ounce) cans black-eyed peas, drained

3   pickled jalapeño peppers, finely chopped

2   tablespoons finely chopped onion

1   (4-ounce) can chopped green chilies, drained

1   garlic clove, minced

1   teaspoon chili powder

1   (8-ounce) package shredded sharp Cheddar cheese

16 tablespoons margarine

Extra shredded sharp Cheddar cheese (optional)

Corn chips

Process peas, peppers, onions, chilies, garlic and chili powder in a blender until smooth. Microwave cheese and margarine, stirring often, until cheese melts. Stir into black-eyed pea mixture. Pour dip into a chafing dish. Sprinkle with extra cheese. Serve hot with corn chips.

Syble's Mexican Dip

MAKES 8 TO 10 SERVINGS

2   (8-ounce) packages cream cheese, softened

1   (16-ounce) can prepared chili and bean dip

½   cup medium hot picante salsa

1   cup shredded sharp Cheddar cheese

1   cup shredded Monterey Jack cheese

½   cup sour cream

½   cup sliced black olives

2   medium tomatoes, chopped

Corn chips

Beat cream cheese with an electric mixer until smooth. Spread ingredients in layers starting with cream cheese, bean dip, salsa, Cheddar and Monterey cheese in a 9 inch quiche dish. Bake at 350 degrees until bubbly. Top with sour cream, black olives and tomatoes. Serve hot with corn chips.

Vidalia Onion Dip

MAKES 4 TO 5 CUPS

3　large Vidalia onions, chopped
　　coarsely

1　garlic clove, minced

2　tablespoons butter

2　cups shredded Swiss cheese

1　cup mayonnaise

2　teaspoons Tabasco sauce

Paprika for garnish

Assorted crackers

Sauté onions and garlic in butter until tender. Remove from heat, stir in cheese, mayonnaise and Tabasco. Pour into a 1½ quart casserole dish. Bake at 375 degrees 20 to 30 minutes. Remove from oven and sprinkle with paprika. Serve warm with crackers.

—— FRAN'S NOTE ——

Crudités: (pronounced cru-di-tay) When serving crudités (raw seasonal vegetables) on a tray, allow 1 tablespoon dip per person (16 tablespoons per cup). 1 cup dip serves 16. One-half gallon serves approximately 90 to 100. Hollow out a green or purple cabbage to hold dip. Elevate the hollowed-out head of cabbage on a tray or basket of greens. Arrange the crudités around the cabbage according to color. The vegetables used on a crudités tray will depend upon the season. Each should be in bite-size pieces. Choose different colors of vegetables such as: radishes, carrots, cherry tomatoes, sweet red peppers, bell peppers, cauliflower, turnips, mushrooms, sliced cucumbers, celery, broccoli and asparagus. Allow a total of approximately 2 ounces of vegetables per guest.

Deb's Bean Dip

MAKES 3½ CUPS

1   (8-ounce) package cream cheese, softened
1   (10-ounce) can bean dip
2   teaspoons Tabasco sauce
Salt to taste
1   cup sour cream
½   cup sliced green onions

½   package taco seasoning mix
1   cup shredded sharp Cheddar cheese
1   cup shredded Monterey Jack cheese
Corn chips

Beat cream cheese with an electric mixer until smooth. Add bean dip, Tabasco, salt, sour cream, onions and taco seasoning. Mix well. Spread half of bean mixture in the bottom of a 13x9x2 inch baking dish. Layer half of Cheddar cheese and half of Monterey Jack cheese. Spread remainder of bean mixture. Sprinkle remainder of Cheddar and Monterey Jack cheeses on top. Bake at 350 degrees 20 minutes. Serve warm with corn chips.

Tomato Bruschetta

MAKES 40 SERVINGS

3   ripe medium tomatoes, peeled, seeded and chopped
1   small onion, chopped
2   tablespoons chopped fresh basil or 2 teaspoons dried

1   garlic clove, pressed
¼   teaspoon salt
¼   teaspoon pepper
3   baguettes
2   tablespoons olive oil

Combine tomatoes and onions in a bowl. Add basil, garlic, salt and pepper and stir well. Slice baguettes into ¼ inch thick slices and arrange in single layer on a baking sheet. Lightly brush baguette slices with oil. Bake at 350 degrees 10 minutes or until lightly browned. Remove from oven, spread tomato mixture on each slice of toast. Serve warm.

Stuffed Cherry Tomatoes

MAKES 24 TOMATOES

1   (8-ounce) package cream
    cheese, softened

1   cup cooked shrimp, chopped

1   tablespoon prepared
    horseradish

¼   teaspoon paprika

1   tablespoon lemon juice

24 cherry tomatoes, hollowed out

Parsley sprigs for garnish

Beat cream cheese, shrimp, horseradish, paprika and lemon juice with an electric mixer until smooth. Use a pastry bag or teaspoon to fill cherry tomatoes. Refrigerate. Garnish each with a sprig of parsley prior to serving.

Pasta-Stuffed Tomatoes

MAKES 24 TOMATOES

3   tablespoons acini di pepe
    (rice-shaped pasta)

¼   cup firmly packed parsley,
    finely chopped

¼   cup grated Parmesan cheese

2   tablespoons feta cheese,
    crumbled

1   tablespoon olive oil

1   tablespoon water

¼   teaspoon dried basil, crushed

⅛   teaspoon garlic powder

24 cherry tomatoes, hollowed out

Alfalfa sprouts (optional)

Cook pasta in boiling water for 6 minutes or until tender. Drain well. Combine parsley, Parmesan cheese, feta cheese, oil, water, basil and garlic powder in a mixing bowl. Stir in cooked pasta. Invert hollowed out tomatoes on paper towels to drain. Place tomatoes, stem end down, on serving plate. Spoon pasta mixture into tomatoes. Cover and refrigerate 8 to 24 hours. To serve, let tomatoes stand at room temperature 30 minutes. Serve on a bed of alfalfa sprouts.

Crab-Stuffed Tomatoes

MAKES 20 STUFFED TOMATOES

20 cherry tomatoes, hollowed out

1 cup crabmeat

4 tablespoons mayonnaise

1 teaspoon Dijon mustard

1 teaspoon dried tarragon

¼ teaspoon salt

Pepper to taste

Invert tomatoes on a paper towel to drain. Combine crabmeat, mayonnaise, mustard, tarragon, salt and season with pepper. Fill cherry tomatoes with a teaspoon of mixture. May be filled 2 hours prior to serving and refrigerated.

Joan's Fried Dill Pickles

MAKES 25 TO 30 SERVINGS

1 (32-ounce) jar dill pickles, sliced and cut into 2 inch strips

1¾ cups self-rising flour, divided

¼ teaspoon cayenne pepper

½ teaspoon black pepper

2 teaspoons garlic salt

3 dashes Tabasco sauce

1 cup beer

Vegetable oil

Dredge pickles in 1 cup flour. Set aside. Combine ¾ cup flour, cayenne, black pepper, garlic salt, Tabasco and beer and mix well. Pour oil into a deep fat fryer to the fill line. Heat to 375 degrees. Dip pickles into batter and fry about 40 seconds until golden brown.

Herb-Stuffed Mushrooms

MAKES 30 TO 40 SERVINGS

1½ pounds fresh button
    mushrooms, rinsed and dried

⅓ cup grated Parmesan cheese

½ cup dry bread crumbs

½ cup grated onion

2 garlic cloves, finely chopped

2 tablespoons chopped parsley

1½ teaspoons salt

¼ teaspoon pepper

½ teaspoon dried oregano

4-8 tablespoons butter

Fresh parsley sprigs or pimiento
    strips for garnish

Remove and chop mushroom stems. Reserve caps. Mix chopped mushrooms with
Parmesan cheese, bread crumbs, onions, garlic, parsley, salt, pepper and oregano.
Stuff mushroom caps with mixture and arrange in a lightly buttered shallow baking
dish. Dot each mushroom with a small amount of butter. Bake at 350 degrees
25 minutes. Serve warm and top with parsley sprig or pimiento strip.

*Dr. John Lining, educated at Leyden University,
made America's first recorded scientific weather
observations from his home at the corner of Broad
and King Streets in 1737. Lining, a friend of
Benjamin Franklin, hoped to establish some
connection between weather conditions and disease
through his studies. He also experimented with kites
in the same manner as Franklin, and was successful
in attracting electricity from a lightning flash.*

Sweet and Sour Meatballs

MAKES 60 MEATBALLS

Sauce

1   (20-ounce) can chunk pineapple, drained, reserve juice

2   cups vinegar

½   cup soy sauce

1½ cups sugar

¼   cup cornstarch

Meatballs

1½ pounds ground beef

1   pound ground pork

1   cup dry bread crumbs

2   garlic cloves, minced

2   eggs

Dash of Tabasco sauce

1   teaspoon ground nutmeg

2   tablespoons cornstarch

2   tablespoons vegetable oil

Sauce

Reserve pineapple chunks. Combine 1 cup pineapple juice with vinegar and soy sauce in a saucepan. In a bowl, mix together sugar and cornstarch. Whisk into juice. Cook and stir over low-medium heat until clear and slightly thickened. Keep warm.

Meatballs

Combine beef, pork, bread crumbs, garlic, eggs, Tabasco and nutmeg and mix well. Shape into small balls and roll in cornstarch. Brown meatballs in hot vegetable oil. Transfer to a 13x9x2 inch baking dish. Top with pineapple chunks. Pour sauce over meatballs. Cover with foil and bake at 350 degrees 30 minutes. Serve hot in a chafing dish with toothpicks on the side.

Beef Turnovers

MAKES 50 TURNOVERS

1½ pounds ground beef, cooked and drained

½ teaspoon cayenne pepper

6 green onions, chopped

4 tablespoons medium picante salsa

¼ teaspoon seasoning salt

¼ cup ketchup

1 (8-ounce) can water chestnuts, chopped

1 teaspoon salt

½ teaspoon chili powder

½ teaspoon garlic powder

50 frozen prepared pastry wrappers, thawed

Vegetable oil

Combine cooked beef, cayenne, onions, salsa, seasoning salt, ketchup, chestnuts, salt, chili powder and garlic powder and mix well. Fill wrappers with a teaspoon full of mixture. Fold and seal according to package directions. Pour oil into a deep fat fryer to the fill line. Heat to 375 degrees. Fry turnovers until crispy and brown. Drain on a wire rack.

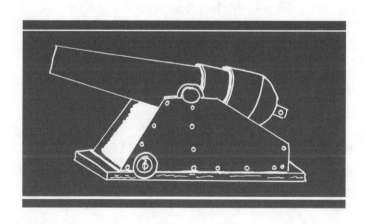

Egg Rolls

MAKES 200 MINI EGG ROLLS

2 (6-ounce) packages vermicelli

2 pounds shrimp, cooked and chopped

2 pounds ground pork, cooked and drained

12 green onions, sliced (including tops)

1 (10-ounce) can bean sprouts, drained

2 (5-ounce) cans chopped water chestnuts, drained

2 (5-ounce) cans bamboo shoots, finely chopped

1 cup finely chopped carrots

2 eggs, beaten

2 tablespoons Worcestershire sauce

4 tablespoons soy sauce

2 teaspoons sugar

1½ teaspoons ground ginger

4 teaspoons salt

1 teaspoon pepper

1 package egg roll wrappers

Vegetable oil

Soak vermicelli in hot water 10 minutes. Drain and cut into small pieces. Combine pasta, shrimp and pork and mix well. Add onions, sprouts, chestnuts, bamboo shoots, carrots, eggs, Worcestershire sauce, soy sauce, sugar, ginger, salt and pepper. Mix until well combined. Make rolls according to wrapper package directions. Pour oil into a deep fat fryer to the fill line. Heat to 350 degrees. Fry egg rolls until golden brown. Drain on a rack. Serve with Sweet and Sour Sauce.

Sweet and Sour Sauce

MAKES 2 CUPS

½ cup vinegar

½ cup water

¼ cup sugar

¼ cup cornstarch

½ cup pineapple juice

Combine vinegar, water and sugar in a saucepan. Bring to boil. In a bowl, blend cornstarch and pineapple juice. Whisk into sugar mixture. Cook, stir constantly, until mixture thickens. Serve with egg rolls.

Petite Wontons

MAKES 24 WONTONS

½ pound mild pork sausage, cooked and drained

½ pound hot pork sausage, cooked and drained

¼ (10-ounce) package frozen spinach, cooked and drained well

1 tablespoon port

1 (8-ounce) can water chestnuts, chopped

1 tablespoon soy sauce

2 tablespoons sliced green onion

¼ teaspoon crushed red pepper

1 package wonton wrappers

Vegetable oil

Sweet and sour mustard sauce

Combine cooked pork, spinach, port, chestnuts, soy sauce, onions and red pepper. Mix well. Spoon 1 teaspoon of pork mixture onto each wrapper. Fold 2 sides of wrapper over filling. Brush exposed part of wrapper with egg white wash (see below). Fold over remaining 2 sides and seal. Pour oil into a deep fat fryer to the fill line. Heat to 375 degrees. Fry wontons about 40 seconds until crisp. Drain on paper towels. Serve with sweet and sour mustard sauce.

FRAN'S NOTE

To make egg white wash, beat together 2 egg whites and 2 teaspoons water.

Rumaki

MAKES 25 SERVINGS

¼ cup soy sauce

1½ tablespoons dry white wine

⅛ teaspoon ground ginger

2 garlic cloves, minced

1 pound chicken livers, cut into 1 inch pieces

1 (8-ounce) can water chestnuts, drained and cut in half

18 slices bacon, cut into thirds

Combine soy sauce, wine, ginger and garlic in a bowl and mix well. Place chicken livers in soy sauce marinade. Cover and refrigerate 2 to 3 hours. Place chestnut half and a piece of chicken liver on bacon piece. Roll up bacon and secure with a toothpick. Arrange livers on baking sheet. Broil 4 inches from heat source 3 minutes on each side or until bacon is crisp.

FRAN'S NOTE

Making Sandwiches

Allow three finger-size sandwiches per person. You will need a one pound loaf of bread and 2 to 3 cups of sandwich filling or 1 pound of thinly-sliced meat. Buy an assortment of natural breads. Some good breads for finger sandwiches are thinly sliced pumpernickel, egg bread, whole wheat, white, dark rye, light rye and dill rye. Spread a thin coating of mayonnaise over both slices of bread before spreading sandwich filling. Trim all crusts from bread and cut into quarters. Using an electric knife to trim crusts and divide into sections is the easiest and most accurate technique.

Vegetable Sandwiches

MAKES 120 QUARTERS

1   cup chopped celery
1   large bell pepper, chopped
2   medium cucumbers, chopped
2   large tomatoes, seeded and
    chopped
2   teaspoons salt
Juice of 1 lemon

2   (¼-ounce) envelopes unflavored
    gelatin
2   cups mayonnaise-type salad
    dressing
2½ loaves sandwich bread
Mayonnaise

Place celery, peppers, cucumbers and tomatoes in a colander resting over a saucepan. Sprinkle with the salt and juice. Allow to drain. Remove colander. Add gelatin to vegetable drippings in a saucepan. Cook, stirring often, over low heat until gelatin is dissolved. Blend in dressing. Stir in vegetables until well blended. Cover and refrigerate for 24 hours or until it becomes firm. Spread one side of each bread slice with a thin layer of mayonnaise. Then spread vegetable filling on one bread slice and top with another bread slice. Trim off crusts and cut each sandwich into quarters

Spinach Sandwiches

MAKES 48 QUARTERS

1   (10-ounce) box frozen spinach,
    lightly cooked
Salt and pepper to taste
1½ cups mayonnaise
¼   cup minced dried onions

¼   cup dried parsley
1   tablespoon fresh lemon juice
¾   teaspoon Tabasco sauce
1   loaf of wheat or white bread

Drain spinach well and dry with paper towels. Season with salt and pepper. Set aside. Combine mayonnaise, onions, parsley, juice and Tabasco. Add spinach and mix well. Refrigerate overnight. Spread spinach filling on bread slices and top with another slice. Trim edges off and cut each sandwich into quarters.

Fran's Chicken Salad for Sandwiches

MAKES FILLING FOR 2 LOAVES OF WHITE
OR WHEAT SANDWICH BREAD

1	(5 pound) whole chicken	2	cups chopped celery
2	tablespoons lemon juice	2	cups mayonnaise
2	teaspoons salt or to taste		

Cover chicken with water in a large stockpot. Bring to a boil and cook chicken until tender. While warm, remove meat from bones, cool and hand chop. Combine chicken with juice, salt, celery and mayonnaise and mix well. Adjust mayonnaise for desired consistency.

FRAN'S NOTE

Whole chickens are available in different sizes to suit the cooking method and the family. We use the roaster, 5 to 6 pounds, to make chicken salad. It yields enough to make two loaves of sandwiches.

Curried Shrimp Sandwiches

MAKES 24 SERVINGS

⅓	cup mayonnaise	¾	cup shrimp, cooked and chopped
1	tablespoon lemon juice		
1	tablespoon apricot preserves	24	slices party rye bread
½	teaspoon curry powder		

In a small bowl, stir together mayonnaise, juice, apricot preserves and curry. Stir in shrimp. Spread on bread to make open-face sandwiches. Cover and refrigerate.

Muffaletta-Style Po-Boys

MAKES 4 TO 8 SERVINGS

2 (10-ounce) packages French rolls, cut in half	6 tablespoons chopped pimiento stuffed olives
¼ cup mayonnaise	4 ounces sliced salami
1 tablespoon pimiento stuffed olive juice	2 tablespoons chopped ripe olives
4 ounces sliced ham	1 (8-ounce) package mozzarella cheese slices

Place rolls cut-side up on baking sheet. Combine mayonnaise and olive juice. Spread on each roll half. Place one slice ham on bottom half of each roll. Top with 1½ tablespoons stuffed olives. Place one slice salami on top of olives. Top with ½ tablespoon ripe olives. Place 2 slices mozzarella cheese on each remaining roll half. Set all roll halves under broiler until cheese melts and is bubbly. Place cheese halves on top of meat halves and slice to serve.

Parmesan Squares

MAKES 120 SERVINGS

2 loaves white sandwich bread	¼ cup plus 2 tablespoons mayonnaise
8 tablespoons butter, softened	
2 (8-ounce) packages cream cheese, softened	6 green onions, sliced
	1 cup Parmesan cheese, grated

Butter one side of each bread slice. Arrange in a single layer on baking sheet and toast. Turn and broil unbuttered side until lightly toasted. Transfer to rack and cool. Combine cream cheese, mayonnaise and onions in large bowl. Spread about 2 teaspoons of mixture over buttered side of bread. Sprinkle with Parmesan cheese. Trim crusts and cut into bite size squares. Electric knife works best. May be frozen at this point. Arrange bread squares on baking sheet. Broil about 5 minutes until bubbly and golden. Serve immediately.

Miniature Orange Muffins with Turkey

MAKES 24 MUFFINS

1½ cups sugar, divided

8 tablespoons unsalted butter, softened

2 eggs

1 teaspoon baking soda

1 cup buttermilk

2 cups sifted all-purpose flour

½ teaspoon salt

1 cup raisins

Zest and juice of 1 orange

1 pound thinly sliced smoked turkey breast, cut into bite-size pieces

Orange marmalade

Preheat oven to 400 degrees and grease two 12 cup miniature muffin pans. Cream 1 cup sugar and butter with an electric mixer until smooth. Add eggs and beat until fluffy. Combine baking soda with buttermilk. Sift flour and salt together. Add dry ingredients and buttermilk, alternately, to creamed mixture. Stir until well mixed. In a food processor, grind raisins and orange zest. Add to batter. Spoon batter into the prepared muffin cups. Bake 12 minutes or until golden brown and firm to the touch. Remove the pans to a baking rack and set close together. Brush the tops with orange juice and sprinkle with ½ cup sugar while still warm. After 5 minutes, turn out from pans. Cool completely before cutting each muffin in half. Place a small amount of turkey on each muffin bottom. Top turkey with ½ teaspoon orange marmalade and cover with muffin top.

Alberta's Bacon and Cheese Squares

MAKES 64 SQUARES

8   slices bacon, cooked and
    crumbled

⅓   cup mayonnaise

1   cup shredded sharp Cheddar
    cheese

1   small onion, grated

1   egg, slightly beaten

¼   teaspoon dry mustard

1   teaspoon Worcestershire sauce

Dash of Tabasco sauce

8   slices day-old bread, toasted

Paprika for garnish

Combine bacon, mayonnaise, cheese, onions, egg, mustard, Worcestershire sauce and Tabasco. Spread mixture over toast. Using an electric knife, trim crust and cut into 4 long strips and then cut again, the opposite way. Sprinkle with paprika. Place squares on baking sheet. Bake at 350 degrees 20 minutes.

FIRST indigo to be planted and harvested in America was grown in Charleston in 1690. Used as a dye, indigo became a much wanted product in Europe, bringing high prices. Some Charlestonians tripled their investment in just two short years, so valuable was this indigo.

Spanakopita

MAKES 160 SERVINGS

1   (8-ounce) package cream cheese, softened

1   pound feta cheese, drained and crumbled

½   cup grated Parmesan cheese

3   tablespoons olive oil

4   eggs, lightly beaten

⅓   cup finely chopped onions

1   teaspoon dried dill

½   teaspoon salt

⅓   teaspoon pepper

4   (10-ounce) packages frozen chopped spinach, thawed and squeezed dry

2   (16-ounce) packages frozen phyllo dough, thawed

2   pounds unsalted butter, melted and cooled

Mix together cream cheese, feta cheese, Parmesan cheese, oil, eggs, onions, dill, salt and pepper. Fold in spinach and mix well. To assemble, place sheets of phyllo on a flat surface. Cut sheets into 6x12 inch strips. Cover pastry with a damp towel to prevent from drying out. Brush half the strip lengthwise with melted butter. Fold in half to make a 3 inch wide strip. Brush top with butter. Spoon a teaspoon of filling onto each strip, 1½ inches from an edge. Fold over the short end of phyllo at an angle to make a seal over filling. Fold remaining length of phyllo strip in alternating triangles. Brush top of triangle with butter. Place triangles on a buttered baking sheet. Bake at 400 degrees 10 minutes or until golden brown.

California Oven-Fried Quesadillas

MAKES 32 SERVINGS

2½ cups shredded Monterey Jack cheese

1 (6-ounce) jar marinated artichoke hearts, drained and chopped

1 (2¼-ounce) can sliced ripe olives, drained

⅔ cup picante sauce

½ cup almonds, toasted

¼ cup loosely packed cilantro, chopped

8 (7-8 inch diameter) flour tortillas

3 tablespoons butter, melted

Additional picante sauce and lime wedges

Preheat oven to 450 degrees. Combine cheese, artichokes, olives, picante sauce, almonds and cilantro in large bowl. Mix well. Brush one side of 4 tortillas with butter. Place buttered side down on baking sheet. Place 1 cup cheese mixture on each tortilla. Spread to within ¾ inch of edge. Top each with remaining tortillas, pressing firmly. Brush tops of tortillas with butter. Bake about 10 minutes or until tops are lightly browned. Remove from oven and cool 3 to 5 minutes. Cut each quesadilla into 8 wedges. Serve with additional picante sauce and lime wedges.

FRAN'S NOTE

For every kind of hors d'oeuvre you serve at your parties, you should always have two trays. One on the buffet table and one in the kitchen that is completely stocked and ready to go. Put the full tray in place as you remove the skimpier one, and the buffet refreshments will always look plentiful. If you do not have enough good trays to do this, beg or borrow what you need or dress up a tattered old tray by lining it with galax or lemon leaves or pittosporum. All of these can be purchased inexpensively from your local florist. Fresh parsley with the stems cut away will hide a worn or unattractive serving tray and also provide a sensible bed for hors d'oeuvres that will not stand upright. It disguises the less-than-appetizing crumbs that are always left behind, as well.

FRAN'S NOTE

Dressed-up votive candles create a beautifully understated display of lights. We place candles in inexpensive holders from the dime store, then wrap the holders in galax leaves, using ⅛ inch ribbon tied with a single tiny jingle bell. Several dozen, streaming down the length of a mantel or massed on a buffet or dining table, will give any room a holiday glow.

Drinks, Glasses, Chilling Wine & Beer
Determining the number of drinks in the bottle:
1 liter alcohol = 22 (1½-ounce) drinks
1 750ml bottle wine = 6 (4-ounce) glasses
1 (1½ liter) bottle wine = 12 (4-ounce) glasses
1 bottle champagne = 6 flute glasses

Types of Glassware:
Old-fashioned glasses (with thick bottoms)
Highball glasses
All-purpose wine glasses
Brandy snifters
Liqueur glasses
Cocktail glasses
Champagne flutes or tulip glasses
Beer mugs or beer pilsners

Red Wine should be served at room temperature (65 degrees) while white wines and rosés are best served chilled. Champagne and sparkling wines should be served cold (45 degrees). Purchase a good wine opener. Beer should be iced down about 1 hour prior to guests' arrival. Allow 2 pounds of ice per person, more in hot weather.

Usually, allow 2.5 beverage servings per person during a 3-hour party. And do not forget to have plenty of cocktail napkins for drinks.

Champagne Punch

MAKES 18 CUPS

2   (1 liter) bottles ginger ale, chilled and divided

1   (6-ounce) can frozen lemonade concentrate, thawed and undiluted

12   maraschino cherries

1   (12-ounce) can frozen orange juice concentrate, thawed and diluted

1   (25.4-ounce) bottle dry champagne, chilled

The day before you plan to serve the punch, pour 1 bottle of ginger ale and lemonade concentrate into an 11 cup ring mold. Add cherries and freeze until firm. Unmold ice ring in a punch bowl. Add second bottle of ginger ale, orange juice and champagne. Stir well.

Syble's Banana Slush Punch

MAKES 72 SERVINGS

4   cups sugar

6   cups water

1   (12-ounce) can frozen lemonade concentrate, thawed and undiluted

2   (12-ounce) cans frozen orange juice concentrate, thawed and undiluted

1   (46-ounce) can pineapple juice

6   ripe bananas, mashed

6   (28-ounce) bottles ginger ale, chilled

Dissolve sugar in water. Add lemonade concentrate, orange concentrate and pineapple juice. Stir bananas into juice mixture and freeze. Remove from freezer and thaw to a slush 2 hours prior to serving. Add ginger ale when ready to serve.

Perfect Hostess Punch

MAKES 25 SERVINGS

2 (10-ounce) packages frozen sliced strawberries in syrup, partially thawed	½ cup lemon juice
	1 (6-ounce) can frozen orange juice concentrate, thawed
3 cups apricot nectar, chilled	1 cup sugar
3 cups cold water	1 (1 liter) bottle ginger ale, chilled

Purée strawberries in a blender until smooth. Combine strawberries, apricot nectar, water, lemon juice, orange juice concentrate and sugar. Stir until sugar dissolves. Pour into a punch bowl. Slowly add ginger ale prior to serving.

Hamby's Golden Fruit Punch

MAKES 50 SERVINGS

2 (46-ounce) cans pineapple juice	1 (6-ounce) box lemon flavored gelatin
2 (12-ounce) cans frozen orange juice concentrate, thawed	2 (2 liter) bottles ginger ale, chilled

Combine pineapple juice, orange juice concentrate and gelatin and mix well. Refrigerate until ready to serve. Pour into punch bowl. Add ginger ale prior to serving.

Marge's Coffee Punch

MAKES 40 SERVINGS

1 quart boiling water	⅔ cup sugar
1 (2-ounce) jar instant coffee	1 gallon vanilla ice cream or more
2 (1-ounce) squares unsweetened chocolate, melted	2 quarts whole milk

Combine water, coffee, chocolate and sugar. Stir until mixed. Chill until ready to serve. To serve, place 1 gallon ice cream and 2 quarts milk in a punch bowl. Slowly pour coffee mixture over ice cream and milk. Blend well. Serves 40.

Spiced Hot Mocha

MAKES 8 SERVINGS

3 ounces semisweet chocolate, cut up	2 tablespoons instant coffee
	2 sticks cinnamon
¾ cup water	2 teaspoons vanilla
2 tablespoons sugar or to taste	Whipped cream (optional)
6 cups milk	

Combine chocolate and water in a large saucepan. Cook and stir over medium heat until mixture is smooth and comes to a boil. Add sugar, milk, instant coffee and cinnamon sticks. Simmer over low heat until thoroughly heated, stirring occasionally. Remove from heat; discard cinnamon sticks. Stir in vanilla. Top individual servings with whipped cream.

Refreshing Orange-Almond Punch

MAKES 40 SERVINGS

2 **cups water**	½ **gallon orange sherbet, softened**
1 **(6-ounce) can frozen lemonade concentrate, thawed**	2 **(2 liter) bottles ginger ale, chilled**
1 **tablespoon almond extract or to taste**	**Oranges slices**

In a pitcher, combine water, lemonade concentrate and almond extract and mix well. Cover and refrigerate. To serve, place scoops of sherbet in a punch bowl. Pour in lemonade mixture. Slowly add ginger ale and stir gently. Garnish with orange slices. Serve immediately.

FRAN'S NOTE

Never place an ice mold in an empty glass punch bowl. The extreme change in temperature will crack the glass bowl when the other ingredients are added. Ice dilutes the flavor of cold punches. Always have the ingredients as cold as possible before adding the carbonated liquid. It also helps to chill the punch bowl in the refrigerator—not the freezer. You may also pre-chill the glasses. If a less sweet punch is desired, use club soda or lemon sour in place of the lemon-lime flavored carbonated beverage or ginger ale. The lemon sour will add some zip to the punch. For a decorative ice ring that will not dilute the punch, freeze fruit juice with some red and green maraschino cherries in an ice mold. Garnish cold drinks with thin slices of lemon or orange slices, cucumbers, bright green or red maraschino cherries, whole fresh strawberries, raspberries or fresh mint leaves.

BREADS, BREAKFAST
AND
BRUNCHES

Faint, Yeasty Smell Remains

In the pre-dawn hours of last Saturday, the last over-night yeast-risen dough went into the oven at 487 Meeting Street and Henry Beckroge closed the doors on a Charleston tradition...

~ *Charleston Evening Post, June 4, 1973*

Uncle Henry, a third generation baker, and I
sit on the front porch of his suburban house,
drinking coffee and craving cinnamon rolls
like the ones he used to make before he
retired, locked the door, sold his store in the
city, leaving faces he can't forget—

brides and their wedding cakes, Europeans
buying dark-rye, ladies calling in orders for
almond macaroons and vanilla cakes to
serve at their parties, kids spending pennies
for Mary Janes, and especially the ones with
empty pockets.

He looks at me, "I didn't know how much I'd
miss them." His smile carries me back to those
days when his hands were busy kneading dough
in the evenings and rising at four in the mornings
to fire-up the wood-burning oven. Those hands
fried donuts the old-fashioned way, dipping them,
one at a time, into a pan of hot oil. Those hands
jellied vanilla cakes and frosted them with chocolate,
cherry, orange and vanilla icing. There were times
I resented the intensity and long hours of his
labor for so little profit, but I treasure the
wealth that "Yeasty smell" has given me.

~ *Elizabeth Bullock Godfrey*

The Old Museum

One of my favorite places to visit was the Old Museum at the corner of Rutledge and Calhoun. The large building was constructed in 1899 for a reunion of Confederate soldiers, and after that was used to exhibit the collection of artifacts that had been moved from place to place since it was founded, in 1773. The exhibits were set up somewhat like a fair, with little rooms or designated areas for specific displays. Close to the entrance was an Egyptian mummy. Toward the back and hanging from the ceiling was the skeleton of the whale that was captured near High Battery. Indian artifacts were exhibited to the left, and the hollowed-stump mortars and huge pestles used to separate the outer hull from the rice grains were located in the upper right mezzanine. Charleston silver, dishes, furniture and clothing were arranged in a little room-like area in the front mezzanine. The fascinating memory that lingers is the orchestrated spaciousness that allowed me to concentrate on one exhibit at a time, yet absorb the entire experience within this " musty" context.

~ *Elizabeth Bullock Godfrey*

Mrs. Mitchum's Angel Biscuits

MAKES 36 BISCUITS

1   package active dry yeast
¼   cup warm water
    (115 to 120 degrees)
5   cups all-purpose flour
1   tablespoon baking powder
¼   cup sugar (save 1 teaspoon to
    mix with yeast)

1½ teaspoons salt
½   teaspoon baking soda
1   cup vegetable shortening
2   cups buttermilk, room
    temperature
½   cup all-purpose flour
½   cup butter, melted

Combine yeast and water until softened. Set aside. Sift together flour, baking powder, sugar, salt and baking soda in a mixing bowl. Cut in shortening to resemble coarse meal. Combine 1 teaspoon sugar with buttermilk and mix with yeast mixture. Add to dry ingredients and blend into a soft dough. Cover and refrigerate at least 3 hours. Sprinkle flour on clean surface. Roll dough to ½ inch thickness and cut with biscuit cutter. Place biscuits on heavily greased baking sheet. Cover and let rise 45 minutes to 1 hour. Bake at 350 degrees 30 minutes or until lightly brown. Brush tops with melted butter immediately after removing from oven.

— FRAN'S NOTE —

Mrs. Mitchum is not only a great bread baker,
but has been making delicious wedding cakes for over 40 years.

Hamby's Buttermilk Biscuits

MAKES 60 SMALL BISCUITS

5 cups self-rising flour
1 tablespoon sugar
1 cup vegetable shortening

2 cups buttermilk
Melted butter

Combine flour and sugar. Cut in shortening with a pastry blender to resemble coarse meal. Add buttermilk. Stir until dry ingredients are moistened. Turn the dough onto a lightly floured surface and knead 4 times. Roll dough to ½ inch thickness and cut with biscuit cutter. Place on lightly greased baking sheet. Bake at 450 degrees 8 to 10 minutes. Brush tops with melted butter immediately after removing from oven. Biscuits may be served plain or filled with premium or country ham.

FRAN'S NOTE

Be sure the oven is set on 450 degrees throughout the baking period. A lower temperature will dry biscuits out before they are done. When turning dough out onto pastry cloth, avoid adding too much extra flour as this will cause the dough to toughen. A shiny baking sheet will help prevent over-browning biscuits on the bottom.

Cream Cheese Biscuits

MAKES ABOUT 18 BISCUITS

1 (3-ounce) package cream
    cheese, softened
8 tablespoons butter, softened

1 cup all-purpose flour
¼ teaspoon salt

Cream together cream cheese and butter. Blend in flour and salt. Form long rolls (2½ inches in diameter) on waxed paper. Refrigerate several hours or overnight. Slice into ¼-inch slices and place on ungreased baking sheet. Bake at 400 degrees 10 minutes.

Syble's Cheese Biscuits

MAKES 50 BISCUITS

2 cups self-rising flour
⅓ cup vegetable shortening

1 cup extra sharp shredded
Cheddar cheese
⅔ cup buttermilk

Combine flour and shortening with pastry blender. Stir in cheese. Add buttermilk and blend until dry ingredients are moistened. Turn out dough onto a lightly floured surface and knead 4 times. Roll dough to ½ inch thickness and cut with small biscuit cutter. Place on a lightly greased baking sheet. Bake at 450 degrees 8 to 10 minutes.

Sweet Potato Biscuits

MAKES 4 DOZEN

1 pound sweet potatoes
5⅓ tablespoons butter
⅓ cup sugar

4 cups self-rising flour, sifted
1 cup shortening
1-2 tablespoons water, if needed

Cook potatoes for 30 minutes in boiling water until soft. Remove skins and mash. Add butter and sugar while hot. When cool, add flour. Cut in shortening and add water to reach desired consistency. Roll dough to ½-inch thickness. Cut with biscuit cutter and place on a baking sheet. Bake at 450 degrees 10 minutes. Biscuits are delicious plain or may be filled with thinly sliced country ham.

Sour Cream Coffee Cake

MAKES 12 SERVINGS

Sugar Mixture

2   tablespoons sugar

1½ teaspoons cinnamon

1   cup chopped walnuts

Cake

16 tablespoons butter or
       margarine, softened

1¼ cups sugar

2   eggs, beaten well

1   cup sour cream

1   teaspoon vanilla

2   cups sifted all-purpose flour

1   teaspoon baking powder

½   teaspoon baking soda

Pinch of salt

Powdered sugar, as desired

Sugar Mixture

Combine together sugar, cinnamon and walnuts.

Cake

Cream butter and sugar. Add eggs, sour cream, vanilla, flour, baking powder, baking soda and salt. Mix well. Pour half of batter into a well greased 10 inch tube pan. Sprinkle with half of sugar mixture. Pour in remaining half batter. Top with remaining sugar mixture. Bake at 350 degrees 1 hour. While warm, dust with powdered sugar. Cool completely in pan.

Maple-Nut Coffee Twist

MAKES 16 ROLLS

Filling

½ cup sugar

1 teaspoon cinnamon

1 teaspoon maple flavoring

⅓ cup chopped nuts

Glaze

1½ cups powdered sugar

¼ teaspoon maple flavoring

2-3 tablespoons milk

Rolls

1 package hot roll mixture

¾ cup warm water (115 to 120 degrees)

1 egg

3 tablespoons sugar

1 teaspoon maple flavoring

6 tablespoons butter, melted, divided

Filling

Combine sugar, cinnamon, maple flavoring and nuts and mix well. Set aside.

Glaze

Combine powdered sugar, maple flavoring and milk and blend well. Set aside.

Rolls

Remove yeast from roll mix package. Dissolve yeast in water. Stir in egg, sugar, and maple flavoring. Blend in roll mixture. Knead 2 to 3 minutes on a floured surface until smooth and satiny. Place dough in a greased bowl, turning to coat dough ball. Cover with a towel and let rise in a warm place for 30 to 40 minutes until doubled in size. Divide dough into three balls. On lightly floured surface, roll out one dough ball to a 12 inch circle. Place onto greased 12 inch pizza pan. Brush dough with 2 tablespoons melted butter and sprinkle with one-third filling mixture. Take two dough balls and form two more layers, ending with filling. Use a glass to mark a 2 inch circle in center of dough without cutting through. Cut 16

Maple-Nut Coffee Twist continued

wedges from outside edge of dough to center circle marking. Twist each of the 3 layered wedges five times. Place twists on a baking sheet. Cover with towel for 30 to 40 minutes or until dough doubles in size. Bake at 375 degrees 20 to 25 minutes. While warm, drizzle with glaze.

FRAN'S NOTE

This is a recipe that I made for my children
when they were younger and I had more time.

Banana-Oatmeal Muffins

MAKES 12 MUFFINS

8 tablespoons butter, softened	1½ cups all-purpose flour
½ cup sugar	1 teaspoon baking powder
2 eggs	1 teaspoon baking soda
3 ripe bananas, mashed	¾ teaspoon salt
¾ cup honey	1 cup quick oats

Cream butter and sugar. Beat in eggs, bananas and honey. In a separate bowl, combine flour, baking powder, baking soda and salt. Add to banana mixture. Stir in oats. Spoon batter into muffin cups, filling two-thirds full. Bake at 375 degrees 18 to 20 minutes. Muffins freeze well.

FRAN'S NOTE

Muffins and other quick breads will toughen if the batter is over-beaten.
Do not worry if a few lumps remain, they will disappear during cooking.

Almond Muffins

MAKES 24 MUFFINS

Filling

1 (8-ounce) package cream cheese, softened

1 egg

1½ tablespoons sugar

2 teaspoons orange zest

Muffins

16 tablespoons butter

1½ cups sugar

4 eggs

3 cups all-purpose flour

2 teaspoons baking powder

1 cup milk

1 teaspoon almond extract

1 cup chopped almonds, toasted

Filling

Combine cream cheese and egg. Add sugar and orange zest. Blend well.

Muffins

Preheat oven to 350 degrees. In mixing bowl, beat butter and sugar with an electric mixer until light and fluffy. Add eggs, one at a time, beating well after each addition. Sift flour and baking powder together. Add dry ingredients and milk, alternately, to creamed mixture. Add almond extract and fold in almonds. Spoon ¼ cup batter into lightly greased muffin cups. Then spoon approximately 1 tablespoon filling over batter. Top with remaining batter. Bake 15 to 20 minutes or until muffin bounces back when pressed.

Blueberry Muffins

MAKES 14 LARGE MUFFINS

3 cups all-purpose flour	½ cup vegetable oil
1 cup sugar	1 cup milk
4 teaspoons baking powder	2 cups blueberries, rinsed and well drained
1 teaspoon salt	
2 eggs, lightly beaten	

Combine flour, sugar, baking powder and salt. In a separate bowl, whisk together eggs and oil. Stir in the milk. Blend wet ingredients into the dry ingredients until just moistened. Fold in berries. Spoon batter into greased muffin cups, filling three-fourths full. Bake at 400 degrees 20 minutes.

Sweet Potato Muffins

MAKES 30 MUFFINS

⅔ cup canned or fresh cooked sweet potatoes	½ teaspoon cinnamon
4 tablespoons butter, softened	¼ teaspoon ground nutmeg
½ cup sugar	½ cup milk
1 egg	4 tablespoons chopped pecans or walnuts
¾ cup all-purpose flour	¼ cup chopped raisins
2 teaspoons baking powder	Sugar and cinnamon for topping
½ teaspoon salt	

Purée sweet potatoes in food processor. Cream butter and sugar. Add potatoes and egg and beat until well blended. Sift flour with baking powder, salt, cinnamon and nutmeg. Add dry ingredients and milk, alternately, to potato mixture. Add nuts and raisins and mix just until blended. Do not overmix. Spoon into greased muffin cups, filling completely full. Sprinkle with a small amount of sugar and cinnamon. Bake at 400 degrees 25 minutes.

Fran's Orange Muffins

MAKES 24 MUFFINS

Orange Glaze

Juice of 3 oranges

2 cups sugar

Muffins

1 cup sugar	1 teaspoon baking powder
1 cup vegetable shortening	¼ teaspoon salt
2 eggs	¾ cup finely chopped raisins
¾ cup buttermilk	2 teaspoons orange zest
3 cups all-purpose flour, sifted	1 teaspoon vanilla
1 teaspoon baking soda	

Orange Glaze

Combine orange juice and sugar in saucepan and boil for 2 to 3 minutes. Keep warm.

Muffins

Cream sugar and shortening. Add eggs, one at a time, beating well after each addition. Add buttermilk. In a separate bowl, combine flour, baking soda, baking powder and salt. Stir dry ingredients into sugar mixture. Add raisins, orange zest and vanilla and mix well. Spoon batter into muffin cups, filling two-thirds full. Bake at 350 degrees 15 minutes. Remove from oven and dip tops into orange glaze. Cool on wire rack.

Pumpkin Apple Streusel Muffins

MAKES 18 MUFFINS

Muffins

2½ cups all-purpose flour

2 cups sugar

1 tablespoon pumpkin pie spice

1 teaspoon baking soda

½ teaspoon salt

2 eggs, lightly beaten

1 cup canned pumpkin

½ cup vegetable oil

2 cups peeled, finely chopped apples

Streusel Topping

2 tablespoons all-purpose flour

¼ cup sugar

½ teaspoon ground cinnamon

4 teaspoons butter

Muffins

In large bowl, combine flour, sugar, pumpkin pie spice, baking soda and salt. In separate bowl, combine eggs, pumpkin and oil. Add to dry ingredients. Stir until mixture is just moistened. Fold in apples. Spoon batter into greased muffin cups, filling three-fourths full. Sprinkle Streusel Topping over batter. Bake at 350 degrees 30 minutes.

Streusel Topping

Combine flour, sugar and cinnamon. Cut in butter with a fork or pastry blender until crumbly.

FRAN'S NOTE

For apple muffins, substitute applesauce and allspice instead of canned pumpkin and pumpkin pie spice.

Sour Cream Muffins

MAKES 12 MUFFINS

2   cups self-rising flour   1   cup sour cream
12 tablespoons butter, softened

Preheat oven to 350 degrees. Grease 12 one-half cup muffin cups. Sift flour, measure, and sift again. Cream flour and butter. Stir in sour cream. Spoon batter into the prepared muffin cups. Bake 30 minutes or until done. To freeze, cook only 20 minutes, cool and then freeze. To use after freezing, thaw and bake 8 to 10 minutes.

Banana Nut Bread

MAKES 1 LOAF

1¾ cups sifted all-purpose flour   ⅓   cup vegetable shortening
¾   teaspoon baking soda   2   eggs, well beaten
1¼ teaspoons cream of tartar   3   ripe bananas, mashed
½   teaspoon salt   ½   cup chopped pecans
⅔   cup sugar

Sift together flour, baking soda, cream of tartar and salt. Set aside. In mixing bowl, beat sugar and shortening until light and fluffy. Add eggs and blend well. Add dry ingredients and bananas, alternately, to creamed mixture. Beat after each addition until smooth. Fold in pecans. Spoon batter into a well greased 9x5x3 inch loaf pan. Bake at 350 degrees about 1 hour or until cake tester comes out clean.

—— FRAN'S NOTE ——

Applesauce may be substituted for the bananas.

Yogurt Fruit Scones

MAKES 16 SCONES

2½ cups all-purpose flour	¾ cup raisins
2 teaspoons baking powder	1 egg, beaten
1 teaspoon baking soda	1 cup plain yogurt
⅓ teaspoon salt	2 teaspoons lemon zest
½ cup sugar	Milk for brushing on scones
6 tablespoons cold butter, cut into small pieces	

Preheat oven to 425 degrees. Very lightly grease a large baking sheet. Set aside. Sift together flour, baking powder, baking soda and salt into a large bowl. Stir in sugar with your fingers, rub in butter pieces until mixture is crumbly. Mix in raisins. With a fork, stir in egg, yogurt and lemon zest and blend well to make dough that barely holds together. Turn out onto a floured surface. Roll out with a floured rolling pin to about ½ inch thickness. Cut dough with a 1½ inch round cookie cutter. Place rounds 1 inch apart on baking sheet. Brush tops lightly with milk. Bake 10 to 15 minutes or until scones are well risen and golden. Transfer to a wire rack to cool. Split and serve warm with butter.

Campus and Community Collision

In 1970, the College of Charleston became a State College and began phenomenal growth. The intentional care with which a campus of three buildings collided with a pre-Revolutionary community is a tangible expression of Adaptive Preservation. Instead of razing the 18th Century homes, they were utilized as classrooms, administrative offices and dormitories. In this way the integrity of an entire community has been preserved.

~ *Elizabeth Bullock Godfrey*

Golden Hushpuppies

MAKES 30 HUSHPUPPIES

1½ cups cornmeal
½ cup all-purpose flour
1 teaspoon salt
3 teaspoons baking powder
6 tablespoons finely chopped onion

2 tablespoons finely chopped bell pepper
½ teaspoon baking soda
1 egg, beaten
1 cup buttermilk
2 tablespoons sugar
Vegetable oil

Combine cornmeal, flour, salt, baking powder, onions, peppers, baking soda, egg, buttermilk and sugar and mix well. Heat oil to 350 degrees in deep fat fryer. Drop batter by teaspoonful and fry 3 to 4 minutes. Drain on paper towels.

Sister's Corn Bread

2 eggs, slightly beaten
1 cup sour cream
½ cup vegetable oil

1 cup self-rising cornmeal
1 (8-ounce) can cream corn

Preheat oven to 400 degrees. Grease and flour a 9 inch pan. Mix all ingredients together. Pour into prepared pan and bake 25 to 30 minutes. Serve hot.

Novice's Yeast Rolls

MAKES 40 ROLLS

2	eggs, slightly beaten	1	package active dry yeast
⅓	cup sugar	1	cup warm water
1	tablespoon salt		(115 to 120 degrees)
½	cup vegetable shortening, melted	4	cups all-purpose flour

Combine eggs, sugar, salt and shortening. Soften yeast in warm water. Add to sugar mixture. Gradually add flour to form soft dough. Place dough in a greased bowl, turning dough over so top is greased. Cover and let rise for 1 hour. May store in refrigerator until needed but should be removed 3 hours before ready to use. Roll out dough onto a floured surface. Cut with small biscuit cutter and place on baking sheet. Cover rolls and let rise until doubled in size. Bake at 400 degrees 20 minutes or until lightly brown.

FRAN'S NOTE

Line a basket with a large napkin. Fold corners over rolls.
Allow 1 to 1½ rolls per person at each table, depending on the size
of the rolls. Be prepared to bring out more rolls and butter on request.
Rolls may be served warm or at room temperature.

Crusty French Rolls

MAKES 18 ROLLS

1	package active dry yeast	1	tablespoon sugar
¼	cup warm water (110 degrees)	1½	teaspoons salt
¾	cup boiling water	3-3½	cups all-purpose flour, divided
2	tablespoons vegetable shortening	2	egg whites, slightly beaten

Soften yeast in warm water. Combine boiling water, shortening, sugar and salt. Stir until shortening melts. Cool to lukewarm. Stir in 1 cup flour and beat well. Beat in yeast and egg whites. Stir in enough flour to make soft dough. Turn out on floured surface. Knead about 10 minutes until smooth. Shape into a ball. Place in greased bowl, turning once. Cover and let rise in a warm place for about 1 hour until doubled in size. Punch down. Turn once in bowl. Cover and let rise 10 minutes. Shape into 18 round rolls. Place 2½ inches apart on greased baking sheet. Cover and let rise for about 45 minutes or until doubled in size. Preheat oven to 450 degrees. Place large shallow pan on bottom oven rack and fill with boiling water. Bake rolls 10 to 12 minutes on rack above water.

FRAN'S NOTE

Butter rosettes are an attractive way to serve butter for rolls.
To make, soften butter and place in a 12 or 14 inch pastry bag fitted with tube. Line a baking sheet with waxed paper. Pipe out rosettes. Freeze. Store in plastic bags and return to freezer until ready to use.
1 pound of butter yields approximately 50 rosettes.

Elegant Grits Soufflé

MAKES 8 TO 10 SERVINGS

4	cups milk	⅛	teaspoon cayenne pepper
1	cup quick-cooking grits	3¼	cups shredded Monterey Jack cheese
8	tablespoons butter		
1	teaspoon salt	6	eggs, beaten

Preheat oven to 350 degrees. Bring milk to boil in a heavy saucepan. Add grits. Reduce heat and cook until grits thicken. Remove from heat and stir in butter until melted. Add salt, cayenne and cheese. Fold in eggs. Pour grits into a greased 3 quart casserole dish. Bake, uncovered, for 1 hour and 10 minutes or until puffed and golden brown. Serve immediately.

Garlic Cheese Grits

MAKES 10 SERVINGS

1¼	cups quick-cooking grits, uncooked	8	tablespoons butter
1	teaspoon salt	2	eggs
3½	cups boiling water	1	cup milk
1	roll garlic cheese, crumbled	½	cup shredded Cheddar cheese

Cook grits 5 minutes in salted boiling water. Blend garlic cheese and butter into grits. In a bowl, beat eggs and milk together. Stir into grits. Pour grits into a greased 2 quart casserole dish. Bake, uncovered, at 350 degrees 45 minutes. Sprinkle with cheese and bake 10 minutes longer or until cheese melts.

Breakfast Shrimp with Grits

MAKES 4 SERVINGS

Shrimp

¼ cup chopped onion

¼ cup chopped bell pepper

3 tablespoons butter

3 tablespoons all-purpose flour

2 cups small fresh shrimp, peeled

1 cup water or more

Salt and pepper to taste

2 teaspoons Worcestershire sauce

1 tablespoon ketchup

Grits

3 cups water

1 cup quick-cooking grits

1 cup half-and-half

1 teaspoon salt

4 tablespoons butter

Shrimp

Sauté onions and peppers in butter until tender. Add flour and cook 2 minutes. Add shrimp and cook about 3 minutes longer. Pour in water to make a sauce. Simmer 2 or 3 minutes until mixture thickens. Season with salt and pepper and add Worcestershire sauce and ketchup. Serve over grits.

Grits

Bring water to boil. Slowly add grits, stirring frequently. Blend in half-and-half, salt and butter. Cook 15 minutes.

FRAN'S NOTE

For thicker grits, decrease liquid. For thinner grits increase liquid. May add hot water to thin grits.

Quiche Lorraine

MAKES 8 SERVINGS

6 slices bacon

2 small onions, chopped

3 eggs

¾ cup sour cream

¼ teaspoon salt

1 (12-ounce) package shredded sharp Cheddar cheese

1 (9-inch) deep pie crust, baked

Olives for garnish (optional)

Cook bacon and reserve drippings. Crumble bacon and set aside. Sauté onions in drippings and drain. Combine eggs, sour cream, salt, cheese, crumbled bacon and onions. Egg mixture may be stored in a covered dish in the refrigerator overnight or be stored longer in the freezer. Pour egg mixture into pie crust. Bake at 400 degrees 30 to 35 minutes. Garnish with olives. Cut into wedges. Serve immediately.

Easy French Toast Strata

MAKES 8 TO 10 SERVINGS

8 slices day-old bread, cut into cubes

1 (8-ounce) package cream cheese, softened

1 cup milk

10 eggs

1 teaspoon cinnamon

1 teaspoon ground nutmeg

1 teaspoon vanilla

¼ cup packed brown sugar

Maple syrup

Layer bread cubes evenly over the bottom of greased 13x9x2 inch baking dish. Blend cream cheese, milk, eggs, cinnamon, nutmeg and vanilla in a blender until well mixed. Pour mixture evenly over bread. Sprinkle with brown sugar. Cover and refrigerate overnight. Uncover and bake at 350 degrees about 35 to 45 minutes or until golden brown. Serve with warm maple syrup.

Deviled Eggs

MAKES 24 SERVINGS

1   dozen hard-cooked eggs

1   teaspoon seasoning salt or to taste

1   teaspoon Worcestershire sauce

1   teaspoon prepared horseradish

2   teaspoons sweet pickle juice

2   teaspoons prepared mustard

½   cup mayonnaise or more, if needed

½   teaspoon pepper

Sliced pimiento-stuffed olives or dill for garnish

Slice hard-cooked eggs in half, lengthwise. Remove yolks and grate in food processor. Add seasoning salt, Worcestershire sauce, horseradish, pickle juice, mustard, mayonnaise and pepper. Blend well. Adjust mayonnaise to reach desired consistency. Spoon yolk mixture into a pastry bag fitted with a large star tip. Pipe a rosette of yolk mixture into each white half. Garnish with a slice of pimiento-stuffed olive or sprinkle with dill. Store in refrigerator until ready to serve.

Sausage and Egg Casserole

MAKES 10 TO 12 SERVINGS

2   cups milk

6   eggs, slightly beaten

¾   teaspoon salt

1   teaspoon dry mustard

4   slices white sandwich bread, cut into cubes

1   (8-ounce) package shredded sharp Cheddar cheese, divided

1   pound mild sausage, cooked and drained

Whisk together milk, eggs, salt and mustard. Arrange half the bread cubes on the bottom of a greased 13x9x2 inch baking dish. Sprinkle 1 cup of cheese. Layer half sausage on top of cheese. Pour half egg mixture over sausage. Repeat with bread cubes, cheese, sausage and egg mixture. Cover and refrigerate overnight. Bake at 350 degrees 35 minutes.

Overnight Brunch Casserole

MAKES 12 SERVINGS

7 slices French bread, cut into cubes

2 tablespoons butter, softened

1 pound mild sausage, cooked and drained

⅓ cup chopped broccoli

⅓ cup peeled and chopped tomatoes

⅓ cup chopped sweet red pepper

⅓ cup chopped mushrooms

⅓ cup frozen spinach, thawed and well drained

1½ cups shredded sharp Cheddar cheese

5 eggs, beaten

2 cups half-and-half

1 teaspoon salt

1 teaspoon dry mustard

1 tablespoon chopped fresh parsley

⅓ cup sliced green onions

Arrange bread cubes in buttered 13x9x2 inch baking dish. Add sausage, broccoli, tomatoes, peppers, mushrooms and spinach. Top with cheese. Whisk together eggs, half-and-half, salt and mustard. Pour egg mixture over bread, covering thoroughly. Cover with plastic wrap and refrigerate overnight. Bake at 350 degrees 45 minutes or until middle is set and top is brown. Garnish with parsley and green onions. Serve hot.

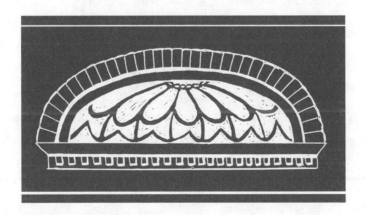

Sissy's Eggs Benedict

MAKES 6 SERVINGS

Hollandaise Sauce

1	egg	3	tablespoons hot water
2	egg yolks	12	tablespoons butter, melted
3	tablespoons lemon juice		

Eggs Benedict

6	slices Canadian bacon	6	tomato slices
1	tablespoon butter		Salt and pepper to taste
3	English muffins, halved and toasted	6	eggs, poached
		18	canned asparagus spears
			Parsley sprigs for garnish

Hollandaise Sauce

Beat egg and yolks until light and fluffy. Add juice and hot water. Cook over low heat, beating constantly, until hot to the touch. Remove from heat and add butter. Beat until thick. Keep warm.

Eggs Benedict

Cook Canadian bacon slices in butter and place on top of toasted English muffin halves. Arrange tomato slices and season with salt and pepper. Add poached egg, then asparagus spears and top with hollandaise sauce. Garnish with parsley sprig.

FRAN'S NOTE

Sissy, a friend from Austria, owned a hotel and restaurant in Austria. She had lunch in our home while visiting the United States and this dish was served. She was so enthralled with this delight that it became a daily favorite in her restaurant.

Golden Hash Brown Casserole

MAKES 8 TO 10 SERVINGS

1 (2 pound) package frozen hash brown potatoes, thawed

1 (10¾-ounce) can cream of chicken soup

2 cups sour cream

1 teaspoon salt

½ teaspoon pepper

1 medium onion, finely chopped

8 tablespoons butter, divided and melted

1 (8-ounce) package shredded sharp Cheddar cheese

2 cups corn flakes, crushed

Combine potatoes, soup, sour cream, salt, pepper, onions and 4 tablespoons butter. Press into an ungreased 13x9x2 inch baking dish. Sprinkle top with cheese and crushed corn flakes. Drizzle remaining 4 tablespoons melted butter on top. Bake uncovered at 350 degrees 45 minutes.

FIRST independent government in South Carolina, and the second in America, was formed in Charleston 1776 in what is now the old Exchange Building at the foot of Broad Street. The assembly authorized the issue of $600,000 in paper money.

Vegetable Frittata

MAKES 10 SERVINGS

2	sweet red peppers, cut into strips	8	slices white bread, cubed and divided
1	yellow pepper, cut into strips	6	large eggs
1	large red onion, thinly sliced	¼	cup heavy cream
2	garlic cloves, minced	1	teaspoon salt
3	tablespoons olive oil, divided	1	teaspoon pepper
2	yellow squash, thinly sliced	1	(8-ounce) package shredded Swiss cheese
2	zucchini, thinly sliced		
1	(8-ounce) can sliced mushrooms	1	(8-ounce) package cream cheese, softened

In a skillet, sauté sweet red and yellow peppers, onions and garlic in 2 tablespoons oil until tender. Remove from skillet, drain and pat dry. Sauté squash and zucchini in 1 tablespoon oil until tender, adding mushrooms for the last 30 seconds. Remove from heat and drain but do not pat dry. Arrange half of the bread cubes on bottom of a 10 inch springform pan. Whisk together eggs, cream, salt and pepper. Stir in cooked vegetables, remaining bread cubes and cheeses. Pour mixture on top of bread cubes lining bottom of pan. Bake at 375 degrees about 25 minutes or until eggs have puffed and the center is set. Be careful not to overcook. Cut into wedges and serve.

SOUPS, SALADS
AND
FRUIT

Rachel

I embrace those Saturdays when I,
a sixth grade helper in my family's
bakery, inhaled early morning aromas
of fresh baked bread and cinnamon rolls
and indulged in afternoon treats of
devil's food cake and almond macaroons.

Down the street, just before dusk, Rachel
picked up her buckets of unsold flowers
and left her place at St. Michael's gate
where she usually sat on an apple crate and
headed for home, stopping at the bakery.

After exchanges of "how are you," Rachel
put her buckets on the floor and bent over,
picking up a bunch of flowers, dripping and
tied together with Spanish Moss, and offered
them to Auntie, in a whisper, "flowers,
flowers," that ended with her voice rising
and eyes widening.

Facing each other with smiles, they built
a bridge with arms, extended in an exchange
of flowers for bread. I stood there, thirteen,
frozen in feelings of pleasure and pain.

~ *Elizabeth Bullock Godfrey*

'Too Poor to Paint...

A friend of mine from Boston told me how he was sent here during WW II to protect Charleston from the enemy. Upon his arrival, he took one look and said, "It looks like the enemy has already taken it." Once called the Jewel in the British Crown, Charleston had declined into a new identity after the War Between the States (often, referred to as the War of the Late Unpleasantness). Now the city was described as 'Too poor to paint and too proud to whitewash.' The spirit of the people was not diminished, however. They knew who they were and that they had homes and buildings of value. So they waited until money became available to make repairs. In the meantime, they polished the brass on their front doors, tended their gardens and opened wide the gates to those gardens, so that others could enjoy the beauty.

~ *Elizabeth Bullock Godfrey*

Steve's and Deb's Favorite Bean Soup

MAKES 8 SERVINGS

2 (15-ounce) cans navy or great Northern beans, undrained

1 tablespoon bacon drippings or olive oil

½ cup chopped onion

1 cup celery, finely chopped

1 garlic clove, minced

2 medium potatoes, cooked and mashed

3 cups water

Salt and pepper to taste

Place beans, bacon drippings or olive oil, onions, celery, garlic, potatoes and water in a 2 quart saucepan. Cook for 30 minutes. Season with salt and pepper.

Ground Beef Vegetable Soup

MAKES 10 SERVINGS

1½-2 pounds lean ground beef

2 quarts water

4 teaspoons salt

¼ teaspoon pepper

1 tablespoon chopped fresh parsley

1 large onion, chopped

1 cup chopped celery

1 (28-ounce) can whole tomatoes, undrained

1 (14-ounce) can whole kernel corn, undrained

1 (8-ounce) can tomato sauce

1 cup sliced carrots

2 potatoes, peeled and diced

4 cups sliced okra

Combine beef, water, salt, pepper, parsley, onions, celery, tomatoes, corn and tomato sauce in large stockpot and bring to a boil. Reduce heat and simmer for 30 minutes. Add carrots, potatoes and okra. Cook 40 minutes longer.

Cheesy Broccoli-Cauliflower Soup

MAKES 8 SERVINGS

3 cups fresh broccoli florets	⅓ teaspoon celery salt
3 cups fresh cauliflower florets	3 tablespoons butter
1 cup sliced carrots	3 tablespoons all-purpose flour
3 ribs celery, sliced	2⅓ cups milk
1 small onion, chopped	1 (16-ounce) box processed
2 cups water	cheese loaf, cubed

Combine broccoli, cauliflower, carrots, celery, onions, water and celery salt in a large stockpot. Bring to boil. Reduce heat, cover and simmer 12 to 15 minutes or until vegetables are tender. Meanwhile, melt butter in a small saucepan. Whisk in flour and cook 4 minutes. Gradually stir in milk and bring to boil. Cook and stir for 2 minutes until thick and bubbly. Reduce heat. Add cheese and stir until cheese melts. Pour into vegetable mixture and heat thoroughly.

FRAN'S NOTE

For best results when cooking with cheese, remember slow and low. High heat and fast cooking causes the fat in cheese to separate, making the cheese stringy and tough. Keep the heat low. After adding cheese to soup or sauce, do not allow the mixture to boil. Instead, stir gently over low heat and the cheese will melt quickly and evenly.

She-Crab Soup

MAKES 12 SERVINGS

8 tablespoons butter	2 teaspoons Tabasco sauce
½ cup all-purpose flour	½ teaspoon ground mace
4 cups milk	1 teaspoon salt
2 quarts half-and-half	½ teaspoon pepper
3 ribs celery, grated	1 cup sherry or to taste
1 small onion, grated	1½ pounds crabmeat
1 tablespoon Worcestershire sauce	

Melt butter in a large stockpot. Whisk in flour and cook 4 minutes until smooth and bubbly. Add milk and half-and-half and bring to boil. In separate pan, sauté celery and onions. Add vegetables to milk mixture and cook 15 to 20 minutes. Add Worcestershire sauce, Tabasco, mace, salt, pepper and sherry. Fold in crabmeat and simmer 5 minutes longer. Do not boil.

FRAN'S NOTE

Roux is a mixture of flour and butter, cooked over
low heat and is used to thicken soups, sauces and gravies.

Gazpacho

MAKES 6 SERVINGS

¼ cup vegetable oil	⅛ teaspoon Tabasco sauce
2 tablespoons lemon juice	¾ teaspoon salt
3 cups tomato juice	⅛ teaspoon pepper
1 cup beef broth	1 bell pepper, finely chopped
¼ cup finely chopped onion	1 cucumber, diced
1 ripe tomato, cubed	Croutons or French bread
1 cup finely chopped celery	

Beat together oil and lemon juice. Stir in tomato juice, broth, onions, tomatoes, celery, Tabasco, salt, pepper, peppers and cucumbers. Cover and refrigerate 4 hours. Serve with croutons or French bread.

FRAN'S NOTE

Croutons add crunch and are a good way to use leftover bread. Prepare a few days ahead to save time and then re-crisp in warm oven. For best results, make with Italian or French bread. Cut bread into uniform cubes. For seasoned croutons, sprinkle with sesame seeds, poppy seeds or garlic powder before baking. Place bread cubes on baking sheet, brush lightly with melted butter and bake in 350 degree oven for 10 to 15 minutes or until golden brown.

French Onion Soup

MAKES 4 SERVINGS

1 tablespoon butter	Salt and pepper to taste
4 medium onions, sliced thin	4 slices French bread, toasted
4 cups beef broth	Swiss cheese, grated
1 teaspoon Worcestershire sauce	

Melt butter in medium stockpot. Sauté onions until brown. Add broth, Worcestershire sauce and season with salt and pepper. Simmer until onions are tender. Ladle soup into ovenproof bowls. Top with toasted French bread and sprinkle with cheese. Place under broiler until cheese melts and is lightly brown.

Toasted French Bread

MAKES 4 SERVINGS

4 slices of French bread, cut ¾ inch thick
Olive oil

Preheat oven to 350 degrees. Place a single layer of bread slices on baking sheet. Bake for 10 minutes until dried and lightly brown. Brush each side with a teaspoon of olive oil. Bake 10 minutes longer.

Old-Fashioned Oyster Stew

MAKES 4 TO 6 SERVINGS

4	tablespoons butter	½	teaspoon salt
12-16	ounces standard-size oysters with liquid	¼	teaspoon pepper
1	quart half-and-half	1	(14-ounce) box oyster crackers

Melt butter in a heavy saucepan. Add oysters and cook over low heat just until edges curl. Slowly add half-and-half and heat gently. Do not boil. Add salt and pepper. Serve steaming hot with oyster crackers.

——— FRAN'S NOTE ———

Soup is a good way to start the meal. Keep first-course soup portions small to avoid spoiling appetites for the remaining courses. Serve in small bowls or cups. Carefully balance the first-course soup with the rest of the meal. For instance, if the entrée contains cream, avoid a creamy soup. Serve a lighter soup with heartier entrées and more substantial soups with a lighter meal.

Southern Potato Soup

MAKES 6 SERVINGS

3 large Russet potatoes, peeled
   and cut into ½ inch cubes
2 (10½-ounce) cans chicken broth
1 medium onion, finely chopped
1 cup half-and-half
Salt to taste

White pepper to taste
1 cup sour cream
6 slices bacon, cooked and
   crumbled
½ cup shredded Cheddar cheese
¼ cup chopped green onions

Combine potatoes, broth and onions in large saucepan. Bring to boil. Reduce heat
and simmer 5 minutes until onions are soft. Stir in half-and-half and season with
salt and pepper. Simmer 20 minutes longer. Add sour cream and heat thoroughly.
Ladle into soup bowls. Top each serving with bacon, cheese and green onions.

FRAN'S NOTE

Top a creamy soup with a crunchy garnish such as croutons,
toasted sliced almonds, pumpkins seeds, thinly sliced carrot or finely
chopped parsley. Pale soups need colorful garnishes such as chopped fresh
herbs, finely sliced green onions or chopped bell or sweet red pepper.

Up-Country Vegetable Soup

MAKES 6 TO 8 SERVINGS

8 tablespoons butter	1 cup canned whole kernel corn, drained
1½ cups shredded carrots	
½ cup chopped white onions	1 teaspoon Worcestershire sauce
½ cup all-purpose flour	1 (8-ounce) package mild shredded Cheddar cheese
3 cups chicken broth	
¼ cup milk	2 tablespoons white wine
2 cups chopped cooked chicken	1 teaspoon salt
	½ teaspoon pepper

Melt butter in a large skillet. Sauté carrots and onions until tender. Set aside. In a large stockpot, whisk flour into broth. Add milk. Simmer over low heat, stirring until smooth. Add cooked vegetables, chicken, corn, Worcestershire sauce, cheese, wine, salt and pepper. Simmer over low heat until cheese melts. Do not boil.

Asparagus, Pear and Walnut Salad

MAKES 4 SERVING

1 (15-ounce) can pear halves, drained and diced	⅓ cup green onions, sliced
	½ cup walnut pieces, toasted and chopped
2 teaspoons fresh lemon juice	
1 pound asparagus, blanched and cut into ½ inch pieces (2 cups)	2 tablespoons honey Dijon mustard
	8 romaine lettuce leaves

In a large bowl, toss pears in lemon juice. Add asparagus, green onions, walnuts and mustard. Toss mixture until thoroughly coated. Place two lettuce leaves on four individual salad plates and spoon asparagus-pear mixture on top. Serve immediately.

Ashley River Bean Bowl Salad

MAKES 12 SERVINGS

Marinade

¾ cup vinegar

¾ cup sugar

2 tablespoons water

1 teaspoon salt

½ teaspoon pepper

½ cup vegetable oil

Salad

1 (17-ounce) can small green peas, drained

1 (17-ounce) can cut green beans, drained

1 (12-ounce) can white shoe peg corn, drained

1 bell pepper, chopped

1 cup finely chopped celery

½ cup sliced green onions

1 (2-ounce) jar pimentos, drained

Marinade

Combine vinegar, sugar, water, salt and pepper in a small saucepan. Bring to boil. Boil 1 minute. Let cool completely. Slowly blend in oil.

Salad

Combine peas, beans, corn, peppers, celery, onions and pimentos in a bowl and toss lightly. Pour marinade over vegetable mixture. Stir gently. Cover and refrigerate overnight.

Syble's Broccoli Salad

MAKES 6 SERVINGS

Dressing

1 cup mayonnaise	2 tablespoons cider vinegar
¼ cup sugar	½ can honey roasted peanuts

Salad

2 heads broccoli, rinsed and cut into small pieces	1 medium red onion, chopped
	9 slices bacon, cooked and crumbled

Dressing

Combine mayonnaise, sugar, vinegar and peanuts and mix well. Refrigerate at least 24 hours.

Salad

Toss together broccoli and onions. Pour dressing over salad at least 2 hours before serving. Top with bacon just prior to serving.

America's first woman pirate, Anne Bonny, was the daughter of an Irish Lawyer who migrated to Charleston when Anne was a baby. She cut a wide swath through the young gentry of Charleston before eloping with a waterfront character named James Bonny to New Providence (Nassau) in the Bahamas, where she apparently associated with such legendary characters as Blackbeard, Stede Bonnet and Calico Jack. She then teamed up with another woman freebooter, Mary Read. Anne Bonny was granted clemency by Bahamian Governor Woodes Rogers, who promised pardons to all who would take an oath renouncing piracy. One story has her later marrying a ship's surgeon and sailing with him for Virginia, never to be heard from in America again.

Sweet and Sour Broccoli Salad

MAKES 10 SERVINGS

Dressing

1 cup mayonnaise	2 teaspoons vinegar
⅓ cup sugar	½ cup finely chopped onion

Salad

2 heads broccoli, rinsed and cut into small florets	½ cup raisins
1 cup shredded Cheddar cheese	8 slices bacon, cooked and crumbled (optional)
¾ cup sunflower seeds	

Dressing

Combine mayonnaise, sugar, vinegar and onions and mix well.

Salad

Combine broccoli, cheese, sunflower seeds, raisins and bacon in a bowl. Pour dressing over salad and gently toss.

Cucumber and Red Onion Salad

MAKES 6 SERVINGS

¼ cup sugar	1 cup water
1 teaspoon pepper	3 medium cucumbers, peeled and sliced into ¼ inch slices
2 teaspoons seasoning salt	1 red onion, thinly sliced
¼ cup vegetable oil	
1 cup white vinegar	

Combine sugar, pepper, salt, oil, vinegar and water and mix well. Mix together cucumbers and onions in a bowl. Pour marinade over salad. Cover and marinate for 1 hour.

Marinated Coleslaw

MAKE 10 SERVINGS

Dressing

⅔ cup cider vinegar

⅔ cup sugar

1½ teaspoons salt

¼ teaspoon pepper

2 teaspoons celery seed

1 (¼-ounce) envelope unflavored gelatin

⅔ cup vegetable oil

Salad

2 small heads cabbage, shredded, about 8 cups

1 small onion, finely chopped

1 cup chopped bell pepper

1 cup chopped sweet red pepper

2 small carrots, shredded

Dressing

Combine vinegar, sugar, salt, pepper and celery seed in a small saucepan. Bring to boil over medium heat. Stir in gelatin until dissolved. Allow to cool. Gradually, whisk in oil.

Salad

Combine cabbage, onions, peppers and carrots. Pour dressing over vegetables and mix well. Cover and refrigerate. Toss gently prior to serving. May store in refrigerator for several days.

FRAN'S NOTE

The gelatin preserves the crispness. Do not mold the slaw.

To double the recipe, use a very large head of cabbage and a medium onion. Double all other ingredients.

Fresh Mozzarella-Tomato-Basil Salad

MAKES 10 SERVINGS

¾ **pound fresh mozzarella cheese**

4 **medium tomatoes, sliced**

½ **teaspoon salt**

¼ **teaspoon pepper**

4 **tablespoons olive oil**

½ **cup fresh basil, chopped**

Fresh whole basil leaves for garnish

Remove cheese from brine and cut into 24 slices. Sprinkle tomato slices evenly with salt and pepper. Alternate tomato and cheese slices on a serving platter. Drizzle with oil. Cover and refrigerate for 4 hours. Prior to serving, sprinkle with chopped basil. Garnish with whole fresh basil leaves.

FRAN'S NOTE

Fresh mozzarella is a soft, white cheese available at gourmet grocery stores or cheese shops. It is sometimes packed in brine, a saltwater solution used for preserving foods.

America's FIRST regularly-scheduled train offering passenger service originated from Charleston in 1830. In 1833 the "Best Friend", the line's steam-powered locomotive, was described by a newspaper article as "flying on the wings of the wind, annihilating space and leaving all the world behind at the fantastic speed of 15 m.p.h." to such distant places as Hamburg, S.C. (just across the Savannah River from Augusta, Ga.)...making the line the world's longest at the time. Part of the wreckage of the Best Friend was used in 1861 to cast the FIRST cannon to be built in the Confederate states, one of which is on display at the Confederate Museum in the old City Market Hall.

Hot German Potato Salad

MAKES 6 SERVINGS

6   medium Russet potatoes

6   slices bacon, chopped

2   tablespoons finely chopped
    onions

¼   cup beef broth

¼   cup vinegar

1   teaspoon salt

2   teaspoons sugar

¼   teaspoon ground black pepper

1   tablespoon finely chopped
    parsley

Cook potatoes in skins in a large pot of boiling water until fork tender. Peel and slice while hot. Keep warm in a bowl. Fry bacon in a saucepan until crisp. Add onions and cook for 3 minutes, stirring constantly. Do not drain. Add broth, vinegar, salt, sugar and pepper to bacon mixture. Bring to boil. Remove and pour over hot sliced potatoes. Gently toss until mixed. Garnish with parsley. Serve warm or hot.

Picnic Potato Salad

MAKES 12 SERVINGS

8   large Russet potatoes, peeled
    and cubed

1   cup mayonnaise or more

2   tablespoons Dijon mustard

¼   cup chopped onion

¼   cup chopped bell pepper

¼   cup pickle relish, drained

¼   cup chopped pimiento, drained

½   teaspoon celery seeds

2   hard-cooked eggs, peeled and
    chopped

Salt and pepper to taste

Cook potatoes in a large pot of boiling water until tender. Meanwhile, combine mayonnaise, mustard, onions, peppers, relish, pimientos, celery seeds and eggs. When potatoes are cooked, drain and transfer to a large bowl. Season with salt and pepper. When potatoes are cool, add mayonnaise mixture and gently toss until mixed.

Garden Rice Salad

MAKES 8 TO 10 SERVINGS

1   (6-ounce) package long grain
     wild rice mix
1   cup diced celery
¾   cup diced tomatoes
½   cup diced cucumbers
2   tablespoons dried parsley
½   teaspoon salt

¼   teaspoon pepper
¾   teaspoon curry powder
½   cup mayonnaise
¼   cup sour cream
½   cup peanuts, toasted and
     chopped

Prepare rice according to package directions, omitting the butter. Transfer rice to a bowl and cool. Add celery, tomatoes, cucumbers, parsley, salt, pepper and curry. In a separate bowl, blend together mayonnaise and sour cream. Add to rice and mix well until coated. Cover and refrigerate overnight. Top with peanuts prior to serving.

Curried Rice and Artichoke Salad

MAKES 8 SERVINGS

1   (8-ounce) package yellow rice
     mix
1   (14-ounce) can artichoke
     hearts, drained and coarsely
     chopped
½   cup bottled garlic dressing
½   cup mayonnaise

6   green onions with tops, sliced
¾   cup chopped bell pepper
½   cup sliced green olives
½   teaspoon salt
¼   teaspoon pepper
½   teaspoon curry powder or to
     taste

Prepare rice according to package directions. Cool rice. Place artichokes in a bowl. Blend garlic dressing and mayonnaise. Pour over artichokes. Add cooled rice and gently toss. Add onions, peppers, olives, salt, pepper and curry and toss until mixed

Spinach and Boston Lettuce
with Raspberry Vinaigrette

MAKES 6 SERVINGS

¾ cup vegetable oil

¼ cup raspberry vinegar

2 tablespoons honey

2 teaspoons Dijon mustard

2 teaspoons poppy seeds

Coarsely ground black pepper to
taste

Salt to taste

1 (10-ounce) head Boston
lettuce, washed, dried, torn
into bite-sized pieces

3 ounces fresh baby spinach,
rinsed and dried

¼ cup walnuts, toasted and
coarsely chopped

In food processor, blend oil, vinegar, honey, mustard, poppy seeds, pepper and
salt for 10 seconds until smooth. Place lettuce and spinach in a salad bowl. Drizzle
half of the vinaigrette over greens and gently toss. Refrigerate remaining dressing
for later use. Sprinkle with walnuts and serve immediately.

Exotic Spinach Salad

MAKES 4 SERVINGS

⅓ cup vegetable oil

3 tablespoons red wine vinegar

1 teaspoon sugar

½ teaspoon salt

¼ teaspoon pepper

1 (10-ounce) bag fresh spinach,
rinsed, dried, stemmed and
torn into bite-size pieces

½ pint fresh strawberries, sliced

3 kiwis, peeled and sliced

½ cup walnuts, toasted and
chopped

Combine oil, vinegar, sugar, salt and pepper in a small jar with lid. Seal tightly and
shake well. Just before serving, gently toss spinach with half of the dressing in a
large bowl. Divide spinach among four salad plates. Arrange strawberries, kiwis
and walnuts over spinach. Drizzle additional dressing over fruit.

Chicken Salad with Pineapple and Almonds

MAKES 6 SERVINGS

1 cup mayonnaise

2 tablespoons Durkee's sauce

2 tablespoons lemon juice

¼ teaspoon pepper

1 cup chopped celery

4 boneless, skinless chicken breast
   halves, cooked and cubed

1 cup pineapple chunks, drained
   (fresh or canned)

½ cup almonds, toasted

Curry powder to taste

Lettuce leaves, rinsed, drained and
   dried

Combine mayonnaise, sauce, juice, pepper and celery and mix well. Stir in chicken until coated. Add pineapple, almonds and season with curry. Serve over a bed of lettuce leaves.

FRAN'S NOTE

Colonial women were dependent upon trade ships to bring prized pineapples from the Caribbean for festive Christmas cooking. Today, you will find an abundance of fresh pineapples at the grocery store, but choosing a truly ripe one can still be a treasure hunt. The most certain test of ripeness is to pluck some leaves from the crown. They should pull out easily. The more fragrant and heavy pineapples will be juicy and fully ripe. When choosing a fine specimen for decoration only, favor the greener pineapple. It will last much longer.

Abbapoola Creek Macaroni-Shrimp Salad

MAKES 10 TO 12 SERVINGS

2 cups dry macaroni or small pasta shells, cooked and drained
1 medium rib celery, chopped
1 small onion, minced
½ cup sweet pickle relish, drained

⅔ cup mayonnaise
2 tablespoons rice vinegar
1½ teaspoons salt
¼ teaspoon pepper
1½ pounds shrimp, peeled, deveined and cooked

Combine pasta, celery, onions, relish, mayonnaise, vinegar, salt, pepper and shrimp in a large bowl and mix well. Cover and refrigerate overnight.

Steve's Shrimp Salad

MAKES 8 TO 10 SERVINGS

1 cup mayonnaise
1½ tablespoons Dijon mustard
Juice of half lemon
1½ teaspoons seasoning salt
½ teaspoon Old Bay Seasoning
1 cup chopped celery

¼ cup chopped onion
¾ cup chopped hard-cooked egg
3 pounds shrimp, peeled, deveined and cooked
Salt to taste

Combine mayonnaise, mustard, juice, salt and seasoning in a bowl. Add celery, onions and eggs. Pat dry the cooked shrimp. Lightly sprinkle shrimp with salt. Add to mayonnaise mixture and mix well

Shrimp Salad

MAKES 3 CUPS OF SALAD OR

ENOUGH TO MAKE 1 LOAF OF SHRIMP SALAD SANDWICHES

2½ pounds shrimp, peeled, deveined, cooked and coarsely chopped

2½ teaspoons salt

2 tablespoons lemon juice

½ teaspoon minced onions

1 cup chopped celery

½ teaspoon celery seeds

1 teaspoon Tabasco sauce

1 cup mayonnaise or enough to bind the mixture

Combine shrimp, salt and juice in a bowl. Add onions, celery, celery seeds, Tabasco and mayonnaise. Serve as a salad or use mixture to make shrimp salad sandwiches.

Shrimp and Crabmeat Salad

MAKES 8 SERVINGS

1 pound fresh crabmeat, picked over

1 pound shrimp, peeled, deveined, cooked and chopped

½ cup chopped bell pepper

¼ cup finely chopped onion

1½ cups finely chopped celery

½ teaspoon salt

1 tablespoon Worcestershire sauce

1 cup mayonnaise

Lettuce leaves

Combine crabmeat, shrimp, peppers, onions and celery in a bowl. Blend salt, Worcestershire sauce and mayonnaise in a separate bowl. Stir into seafood mixture. Serve over lettuce leaves.

Ambrosia Salad

MAKES 12 SERVINGS OR MORE

1½ cups orange juice

¼ cup powdered sugar or to taste

7 large oranges, peeled and cut crosswise into ½ inch slices, reserve juice

5 medium bananas, cut into ½ inch slices

1 (3½-ounce) can flaked coconut

1 (16-ounce) jar maraschino cherries, drained

1 (20-ounce) can pineapple chunks, drained

10 maraschino cherries with stems for garnish

Combine juice and powdered sugar, stirring well. Set aside. Dip banana slices in reserved orange juice to prevent browning. In a trifle bowl, arrange half of orange slices. Top with banana slices, half of coconut, maraschino cherries and pineapple chunks. Top with remaining orange slices. Pour sugar mixture over fruit. Cover and refrigerate. Sprinkle with remaining coconut and garnish with cherries before serving.

— FRAN'S NOTE —

Remove the white layer of skin just under the orange peel.
If not removed, the skin will add a bitter taste. A citrus knife works well in sectioning fruits. The knife has two blades. One separates the sections from the membrane, the other separates the sections from the rind. It is easy to use and is especially helpful in making fruit cups.

Nutty Apple Salad

MAKES 12 SERVINGS

2 cups cubed apple
2 cups thinly sliced celery
2 cups halved seedless grapes
1 cup miniature marshmallows
⅓ cup cold evaporated milk
½ teaspoon sugar

¼ teaspoon vanilla
3 tablespoons mayonnaise
2 tablespoons peanut butter
½ cup mixed nuts
½ cup heavy cream, whipped

In a large bowl, combine apples, celery, grapes and marshmallows. In a chilled mixing bowl, beat milk until frothy. Add sugar and vanilla. Beat in mayonnaise and peanut butter. Add to apple mixture and mix well. Stir in nuts and whipped cream prior to serving.

Kahlúa Fruit Dip

MAKES 4 CUPS

¾ cup packed brown sugar
⅓ cup Kahlúa
1 (8-ounce) package cream
      cheese, softened

1 cup whipped topping, thawed
1 cup sour cream

Cook brown sugar and Kahlúa in saucepan over medium heat until sugar melts. Cool. Beat cream cheese and whipped topping until smooth. Fold into Kahlúa mixture. Gently stir in sour cream. Refrigerate until ready to serve.

Holiday Cranberry Salad

MAKES 12 SERVINGS

1   (3-ounce) package strawberry
   flavored gelatin

1   (3-ounce) package raspberry
   flavored gelatin

2   cups boiling water

1   (10-ounce) package sliced
   frozen strawberries, thawed

1   (20-ounce) can crushed
   pineapple, undrained

1   (16-ounce) can whole berry
   cranberry sauce

1   cup chopped celery

1   cup chopped pecans

Lettuce leaves

Prepare gelatin according to package directions. Cool in the refrigerator until slightly thickened. Add strawberries, pineapple, cranberry sauce, celery and pecans. Pour mixture into a greased 6 cup mold. Cover and refrigerate until firm. Unmold onto a lettuce covered serving platter.

FRAN'S NOTE

To unmold a gelatin salad easily, coat the mold with a thin coating of mayonnaise or cooking spray before pouring in the mixture. When unmolding, put 3 or 4 drops of water on serving platter. This will allow you to move the gelatin to the center of platter.

Sour Cream Fruit Dip

MAKES 2 ½ CUPS

4   tablespoons butter

⅓   cup packed light brown sugar

2   cups sour cream

1   tablespoon vanilla

Melt butter in saucepan. Stir in brown sugar. Cook over low heat until sugar dissolves. Cool slightly. Whisk in sour cream until smooth. Stir in vanilla.

Marguerite's Salad à la Orange

MAKES 4 SERVINGS

Dressing

1½ cups peanut oil
2 tablespoons vinegar
¼ teaspoon salt

¼ teaspoon pepper
½ teaspoon sugar or to taste
Juice from 1 can Mandarin oranges

Salad

4 cups bite-size pieces of romaine lettuce
2 (11-ounce) cans Mandarin oranges, reserve juice from 1 can

1 cup sliced almonds
1 cup raisins

Dressing

Combine oil, vinegar, salt, pepper, sugar and juice and mix well. Set aside.

Salad

Combine lettuce, oranges, almonds and raisins in a serving bowl. Drizzle with dressing.

Cold Sherried Fruit

MAKES 25 SERVINGS

2   cups strawberries, cut into halves

2   cups watermelon balls

2   cups cantaloupe balls

1   cup fresh peeled and sliced peaches

1   cup fresh pineapple chunks

1   cup white seedless grapes

½   cup sherry

1   teaspoon orange zest, minced

½   cup sugar or to taste

1   teaspoon ground coriander

Combine strawberries, watermelon, cantaloupe, peaches, pineapple and grapes in a large bowl and mix well. In a small bowl, combine sherry, zest, sugar and coriander and mix well. Pour sauce over fruit. Cover and refrigerate. Serve with toothpicks.

Pineapple Bake

MAKES 8 SERVINGS

2   (20-ounce) cans sliced pineapple

1   (8-ounce) package shredded sharp Cheddar cheese

⅔   cup sugar

⅓   cup all-purpose flour

1   cup cracker crumbs

4   tablespoons butter or margarine, melted

Drain sliced pineapple, reserving ⅓ cup juice. Place pineapple in a slightly greased 11x7x1½ inch baking dish. Top with cheese. Combine reserved pineapple juice, sugar and flour and mix well. Pour over cheese. Mix together cracker crumbs and butter and sprinkle on top. Bake at 350 degrees 25 minutes or until bubbly.

Fruit Kabobs

MAKES 6 SERVINGS

12 (10-inch) wooden skewers

½ medium cantaloupe, scooped into balls

¼ medium honeydew, scooped into balls

¼ medium fresh pineapple, cut into chunks

1 cup strawberries, rinsed and hulled

18 seedless red grapes

1 tablespoon honey

1 tablespoon lime juice

Thread fruit onto skewers in an alternating pattern. Blend together honey and lime juice and brush onto fruit. Refrigerate until ready to serve.

— FRAN'S NOTE —

When purchasing cantaloupe or honeydew melon, if they do not have a fresh look and do not smell sweet, usually they are not worth buying. A honeydew melon is ripe when you press your thumb on the rounded end and it makes a slight indentation.

When strawberries are in season, you can pick them at local fields or you can buy them at produce stands or at farmers' markets. Look for berries that are plump, bright red and topped with caps of tiny green leaves. Do not rinse them until they are ready to be used. Store berries in an airtight container in the refrigerator, where they will keep for up to two days.

 **ENTRÉES**

Supper Time

The kitchen table, my grandmother's
round oak, handed down to mom, then
me in 1953, spread for supper in front
of a window that frames the remains
of a duck blind, out there in the marsh,

where hunters once hid and waited
beneath a cover of bulrush and brush
hoping ducks would hear their call.
A Great Blue Heron, our daily guest,
makes a grand entrance, fastening

his feet on the duck blind, as if he were
the overseer of this once-prosperous rice field.
Minnows are swept by the tide into
the marsh, where Snowy White Egrets
make smooth landings for their feeding.

Their slender necks bend and bow, then rise
like lilies in bloom, pure, white, against a field
of green. Nets, full of shrimp are pulled from
the river while cackling Marsh Hens hunt high

ground and Cardinals fade into silence. God's
bounty has fed our bodies and his beauty
has nourished our souls... "Let the people
praise you, O God." Amen.

~ *Elizabeth Bullock Godfrey*

Tent City

The earthquake of 1886 brought walls down and sent debris flying. Not only were buildings shaken, but people, as well. Many people had to leave their homes and seek shelter in tents, which had been erected in Washington Park, next to City Hall.

Fifty years later, when I was in the first grade, people were still talking about this frightening time. A friend of mine told me how some of his family came to Charleston from Holly Hill to see the devastation. At the tent city this agonizing prayer was heard:

> *"Dear Lord, you please come down here, yourself.*
> *Don't send your Son.*
> *This is too big a problem to send your Son.*
> *You come, yourself."*

> ~ *Elizabeth Bullock Godfrey*

Power of Benevolence

Etched in stone, above the entrance to the Confederate Home at 62 Broad Street, are these words:

> *Ruined by the earthquake 1886*
>
> *Restored by the people of the Union 1887*

I have pondered these words many times and am amazed by their impact. As news of Charleston's earthquake spread, within a year's time, enough money came in from all over to help rebuild the ruined city. The healing power of benevolence was at work.

> ~ *Elizabeth Bullock Godfrey*

Chili for Working Moms

MAKES 8 SERVINGS

2	pounds ground beef	1	garlic clove, minced or ¼ teaspoon garlic powder	
1½	teaspoons salt			
1½	teaspoons pepper	1	medium onion, chopped	
1½-3	teaspoons chili powder	1	cup water	
		2	(8-ounce) cans tomato sauce	

Combine beef, salt, pepper, chili powder, garlic, onions and water in a heavy skillet. Cook until beef is brown and onions turn transparent. Add tomato sauce and simmer 30 minutes to 1 hour. This is especially good served with rice and a green salad for a quick and easy meal.

VARIATION

Add 1 (15-ounce) can kidney beans, rinsed and drained, to mixture, the last 10 minutes of cooking.

Crock-Pot Beef Stroganoff

MAKES 10 SERVINGS

2 pounds top sirloin steak, cut into cubes

2 tablespoons vegetable oil

2 medium onions, chopped

2 garlic cloves, minced

1 (8-ounce) can sliced mushrooms, drained

1 teaspoon salt or to taste

½ teaspoon pepper

1 cup beef broth

3 tablespoons tomato paste

1½ cups sour cream

4 tablespoons all-purpose flour or cornstarch

Cooked noodles or rice

Dust meat with flour and season with salt and pepper. Brown in hot oil. Remove meat and sauté onions, garlic and mushrooms until onions are golden. Transfer vegetables to crock pot. Add meat, salt, pepper, broth, tomato paste, sour cream and flour to crock pot. Stir thoroughly. Cover and cook 6 hours on low heat. Serve over noodles or rice.

In 1736, America's first fire insurance company—the "Friendly Society for the Mutual Insuring of Houses Against Fire"—was organized in Charleston. Small metal plaques called fire marks were used to identify building to be saved in case of fire. The devastating fire of 1740, which burned more than 300 of the city's buildings, bankrupted the company.

Lasagna

MAKES 10 TO 12 SERVINGS

2	pounds ground beef	1	teaspoon oregano
1	onion, chopped	1	teaspoon salt
1	garlic clove, minced	1	pound ricotta cheese
2	tablespoons vegetable oil	2	eggs, well beaten
2	(16-ounce) cans crushed tomatoes	8	ounces lasagna noodles
1	(6-ounce) can tomato paste	2	(8-ounce) packages mozzarella cheese slices
1	(8-ounce) can tomato sauce	1	cup grated Parmesan cheese

In large heavy pan, lightly brown beef, onions and garlic in oil. Add tomatoes, paste, sauce, oregano and salt. Simmer uncovered, stirring occasionally, about 15 minutes. In a bowl, mix ricotta cheese with eggs. Meanwhile, cook lasagna noodles according to package directions. Drain. Spread about 1 cup sauce in the bottom of a 13x9x2 inch baking dish Then alternate layers of lasagna noodles, sauce, ricotta mix, mozzarella and Parmesan cheese, ending with sauce. Bake at 350 degrees 40 to 50 minutes until bubbly.

Annie and Alfred

My family sent me to visit a neighbor when I was 10 or 11. I don't remember the exact nature of my visit, whether it was to take food or to check on her since we hadn't seen her in a few days, but I do remember that visit with Annie. She lived in a little alley with her son, Alfred, a little younger than I. We knew they had a "hard time making ends meet," but I didn't know how hard until I went inside her one room house. I sat on the bed while she sat in a chair and there was no sheet-rock or finished walls — only newspaper tucked into the cracks or tacked on the inside of the siding.

~ Elizabeth Bullock Godfrey

All-Day Italian Spaghetti Sauce

MAKES 16 SERVINGS

3 pounds ground beef

⅓ pound pork sausage

4 large onions, chopped

2 garlic cloves, minced

3 tablespoons vegetable oil

3 (28-ounce) cans whole tomatoes

4 (8-ounce) cans tomato sauce

2 (6-ounce) cans tomato paste

½ teaspoon ground nutmeg

½ teaspoon cinnamon

½ teaspoon sage

¼ teaspoon ground allspice

1 teaspoon onion salt

1 teaspoon sugar

½ teaspoon pepper

2 teaspoons salt

1 teaspoon chili powder

1 teaspoon Italian seasoning

Hot cooked spaghetti

Grated Parmesan cheese

In a large skillet, brown beef and sausage. Drain. Set aside. Sauté onions and garlic in oil about 15 minutes. Add to meat mixture and mix well. Add tomatoes and tomato sauce. Bring to boil. Reduce heat and simmer over low heat for 3 to 4 hours. During the last hour of cooking, add tomato paste, nutmeg, cinnamon, sage, allspice, onion salt, sugar, pepper, salt, chili powder and Italian seasoning. Serve over cooked spaghetti. Sprinkle Parmesan cheese on top.

Filet of Beef Tenderloin

MAKES 12 TO 14 SERVINGS

1	(5 to 6 pound) beef tenderloin	2	tablespoons browning sauce
2	tablespoons vegetable oil		Coarse black pepper

Have a butcher trim tenderloin and fold meat tail in. Tie in several places with string. Rub meat with oil and browning sauce. Let stand at room temperature for 2 hours. Rub tenderloin with pepper and place in a roasting pan. Roast at 450 degrees 30 minutes. Remove from oven to a rack and lightly cover with tin foil. Let rest 10 minutes before slicing.

FRAN'S NOTE

Beef tenderloin is a popular hors d'oeuvre at our cocktail parties and receptions. This size tenderloin serves 25, served with mayonnaise, horseradish sauce, brown mustard and assorted breads.

Ginger-Honey Flank Steak

MAKES 6 SERVINGS

¾	cup vegetable oil	2	tablespoons minced green onions
¼	cup soy sauce		
2	tablespoons honey	1	garlic clove, minced
2	tablespoons cider vinegar	1	teaspoon ground ginger
		2	pounds beef flank steak

Combine oil, soy sauce, honey, vinegar, onions, garlic and ginger. Pour marinade over steak in a zip-top plastic bag. Refrigerate 3 to 4 hours. Remove from marinade and pat dry. Grill over high heat to desired degree of doneness.

Beef Tenderloin Stuffed with Lobster Tails

MAKES 12 TO 14 SERVINGS

Wine Sauce

½ cup sliced green onions	⅛ teaspoon garlic powder
8 tablespoons butter	½ cup dry white wine

Lobster and Tenderloin

2 (4-ounce) lobster tails	½ teaspoon garlic powder
1 teaspoon salt	Salt and pepper to taste
1 (5 to 6 pound) beef tenderloin, trimmed	1 tablespoon butter, melted
	1 tablespoon lemon juice

Wine Sauce

Cook green onions in butter in a saucepan over low heat until tender, stirring occasionally. Stir in garlic powder and wine. Bring to boil, stirring constantly. Remove from heat.

Lobster and Tenderloin

In a stockpot, combine the lobster tails and salt with enough water to cover. Bring to boil. Reduce heat and simmer, covered, for 5 to 6 minutes or until the lobster meat is opaque. Drain. Remove lobster meat from shell in one piece. Set aside. To prepare beef for stuffing, trim tip ends and slice tenderloin lengthwise, being careful not to cut through bottom and leaving ½ inch on both ends. Rub tenderloin with garlic powder, salt and pepper. Drizzle lobster meat with butter and lemon juice mixture and place down the center of the tenderloin. Secure the tenderloin at 2 to 3 inch intervals with kitchen twine to enclose the lobster meat. Place the tenderloin on a rack in a shallow roasting pan. Roast at 425 degrees 40 minutes or until meat thermometer registers 130 degrees for rare or 140 degrees for medium. Let tenderloin rest for 10 minutes before slicing. Drizzle with wine sauce.

FRAN'S NOTE

This is a must on the menu for the
Hamby family's traditional Christmas Eve party.

Marinated Eye of Round with Horseradish Sauce

MAKES 12 SERVINGS

Horseradish Sauce

1   cup heavy cream

1   cup mayonnaise

Dash of sugar

¼   cup prepared horseradish

¼   teaspoon Dijon mustard

Beef

1   cup soy sauce

⅓   cup gin

1   cup olive oil

4   garlic cloves, crushed

1   (4 pound) eye of round beef
     roast

Horseradish Sauce

Whip cream in a bowl with an electric mixer until soft peaks form. Blend in mayonnaise, sugar, horseradish, and mustard by hand. For a lighter sauce, omit the mayonnaise.

Beef

Combine soy sauce, gin, oil and garlic. Pour marinade over roast in a zip-top plastic bag. Refrigerate for 2 days, turning the roast several times. Remove roast from marinade and pat dry. Place on a rack in a roasting pan. Bake at 350 degrees about 1 hour until meat thermometer registers 140 degrees for medium rare. Remove from the oven and immediately wrap in foil and refrigerate to cool. To serve, slice the meat very thin and serve with horseradish sauce.

Chicken Tetrazzini

MAKES 12 TO 15 SERVINGS

1 gallon chicken broth (saved from boiling chicken to be used to cook the linguini)

1 (10-ounce) can cream of mushroom soup

1½ cups half-and-half

½ cup sherry

1 tablespoon Worcestershire sauce

1⅓ cups freshly grated Parmesan cheese, divided

1 (8-ounce) can sliced mushrooms

1 (8-ounce) can sliced water chestnuts

¼ cup pimiento

8 ounces of linguine, cooked in broth and drained

1½ pounds cooked chicken, pulled or chopped

Salt and pepper to taste

Combine mushroom soup, half-and-half, sherry, Worcestershire sauce, 1 cup Parmesan cheese, mushrooms, chestnuts and pimiento in a bowl. Blend well. Fold in linguine and chicken. Season with salt and pepper. Pour mixture into a greased 13x9x2 inch baking dish. Sprinkle remaining ⅓ cup Parmesan cheese on top. Cover with foil and bake at 350 degrees 40 minutes or until set.

Chicken Tex-Mex Barbecue

MAKES 6 SERVINGS

3 pounds chicken, any pieces

16 ounces favorite barbecue sauce

1 tablespoon packed brown sugar

2 teaspoons prepared mustard

1 teaspoon chili powder

¼ teaspoon liquid smoke

Dash of Tabasco sauce

In a 13x9x2 inch baking dish, layer chicken. Roast at 375 degrees 10 minutes. Combine barbecue sauce, brown sugar, mustard, chili powder and liquid smoke in a small saucepan. Cook and stir over low heat until sugar dissolves. Pour sauce over chicken. Cover with aluminum foil and roast about 40 minutes longer or until done.

Chicken Ambassador

MAKES 6 SERVINGS

6	boneless, skinless chicken breast halves	1	(14-ounce) can artichoke hearts, drained and quartered
1	teaspoon salt	½	pound fresh mushrooms, sliced
	Pepper to taste	1½	teaspoons all-purpose flour
1	teaspoon poultry seasoning	1	can beef broth
8	tablespoons butter, divided	½	cup sherry

Season chicken breasts with salt, pepper and poultry seasoning. Melt 4 tablespoons butter in a skillet over medium heat. Sauté chicken until lightly brown. Combine chicken and artichoke hearts in a 13x9x2 inch baking dish. Melt remaining 4 tablespoons butter in skillet. Sauté mushrooms 5 minutes. Sprinkle flour over mushrooms. Gradually add broth and sherry, stirring until well blended. Simmer 5 minutes or until sauce is thickened. Pour mushroom mixture over chicken and artichokes. Bake, covered, at 350 degrees 45 minutes, adding additional broth as needed to keep chicken moist. Garnish with additional artichoke hearts.

Apricot Chicken

MAKES 6 SERVINGS

6	boned chicken breast halves	½	cup packed brown sugar
2	tablespoons cornstarch	1	cup orange marmalade
¼	cup water	1	cup dried apricots
1	cup orange juice concentrate	½	cup golden raisins
1½	cups apple juice		Hot cooked rice

Layer chicken in the bottom of a greased 13x9x2 inch baking dish. Mix together cornstarch and water in a bowl. Add orange juice, apple juice, brown sugar and marmalade. Mix well and pour sauce over chicken. Bake at 350 degrees 30 minutes. Top with apricots and raisins. Bake 30 minutes longer. Serve hot over rice.

Chicken Curry

MAKES 4 SERVINGS

3 tablespoons margarine
¼ cup chopped onion
¼ cup chopped bell pepper
1½ teaspoons curry powder
⅛ teaspoon ground ginger
1 apple, chopped
1 teaspoon salt
3 tablespoons all-purpose flour
1 cup milk

1 cup chicken broth
2 cups chopped chicken
1 teaspoon lemon juice
Hot cooked rice
Garnish with any of the following:
    4 slices cooked and crumbled bacon, 1 cup raisins, ½ jar mango chutney, ½ cup toasted coconut or ½ cup chopped peanuts

Melt margarine in skillet and sauté onions and peppers. Add curry, ginger, apples, salt, flour, milk and broth. Add chicken and lemon juice. Pour mixture into a 1½ quart casserole dish and bake at 350 degrees 25 minutes. Serve over rice. Garnish with condiments, if desired.

Apricot Glazed Cornish Hens

MAKES 4 SERVINGS

1 cup apricot preserves
⅓ cup fresh orange juice
4 tablespoons butter, melted

4 Cornish game hens, rinsed and pat dry
Salt and pepper to taste

Combine preserves, orange juice and butter to make the glaze. Rub the hen cavities with salt and pepper. Place hens, breast side up, on a rack in a shallow roasting pan, ensuring that they do not touch. Pour glaze over hens. Bake at 350 degrees 1 hour. Baste every 10 minutes or until the hens are very tender. Test for doneness by piercing the skin of the thigh and the juice should run clear. Let stand for 10 minutes before serving.

Chicken and Pepper Pasta

MAKES 8 SERVINGS

6 boneless, skinless chicken breast halves, cut into bite size pieces

Salt and pepper to taste

8 tablespoons butter, divided

1 sweet red pepper, thinly sliced

1 yellow pepper, thinly sliced

1 bell pepper, thinly sliced

1 (8-ounce) package fettuccine, uncooked

3 cups heavy cream

2 tablespoons sherry

1½ cups grated Parmesan cheese

Season chicken with salt and pepper. Melt 2 tablespoons of the butter in skillet over medium heat. Add chicken and sauté 5 minutes or until lightly brown. Remove chicken and set aside. Sauté peppers until tender. Set aside and drain. Cook pasta as directed on package; drain and rinse. To the skillet, add remaining 6 tablespoons butter, cream and sherry. Cook, stirring constantly, until thickened. Return chicken and peppers to skillet. Add hot pasta and Parmesan cheese. Toss and serve hot.

FRAN'S NOTE

Clarified Butter

Cut 16 tablespoons (2 sticks) unsalted butter into small pieces and place in a small saucepan. Melt over medium heat until liquefied. Skim off foam. Slowly pour off clear yellow liquid, leaving behind the residue of milk solids that have settled to the bottom of the pan. Clarified butter will stay fresh in the refrigerator for 2 to 3 weeks and it can be frozen. Makes ¾ cup. When sautéing, try this simple alternative to clarified butter: Heat butter with oil in a ratio of 2 tablespoons butter to 1 tablespoon oil. The oil allows the butter to reach a higher temperature without burning. Butter foams when it is heated. When the foam subsides, the butter is the right temperature for sautéing.

Mediterranean Stuffed Chicken Breast

MAKES 4 SERVINGS

4 (6-ounce) boneless, skinless chicken breasts	1 cup crumbled feta cheese
Olive oil	½ cup sliced black olives
Salt and pepper to taste	3 (6½-ounce) jars marinated artichoke hearts, chopped
¾ cup sliced sun-dried tomatoes in oil, drained	

Pound each chicken breast to about one-fourth inch thickness between sheets of plastic wrap. Place chicken on a baking sheet. Brush with oil and season with salt and pepper. Combine sun-dried tomatoes, feta cheese, olives and artichokes. Spread ½ cup tomato mixture on each chicken breast. Roll each chicken breast, tucking both ends in as you roll. Transfer rolled chicken to a greased 13x9x2 inch baking dish. Top with the remaining tomato mixture. Cover with foil and bake at 375 degrees 40 minutes. Remove foil for last 10 minutes of cooking.

FIRST city in America, and possibly the world, to require pasteurization of milk sold within the city limits was Charleston. Up until 1919, milk was delivered via horse-drawn cart, with each order being dipped out of a large, open container under unsanitary conditions.

Nancy's Champagne Chicken Topped with Shrimp

MAKES 8 SERVINGS

Chicken

8 boneless, skinless chicken breast halves

Salt and pepper to taste

All-purpose flour

4 tablespoons butter

Champagne Sauce

¾ pound fresh mushrooms, sliced

4 tablespoons butter

1½ pounds shrimp, peeled, deveined and uncooked

⅓ cup sliced green onions

2½ tablespoons lemon juice

1 teaspoon salt

¾ cup water

6 tablespoons all-purpose flour

1½ cups half-and-half

¾ cup champagne

1 teaspoon honey or to taste

Chicken

Lightly salt and pepper chicken and dust with flour. Sauté chicken in butter until lightly brown. Place in a 13x9x2 inch casserole dish. Bake at 250 degrees about 15 minutes.

Champagne Sauce

Sauté mushrooms in butter and set aside. In a bowl, combine the shrimp, green onions, juice, and salt. Sauté shrimp mixture over medium heat until shrimp turns pink. Remove shrimp with a slotted spoon and set aside. Reserve shrimp liquid. In a small bowl, combine water and flour. Add to hot shrimp liquid in the skillet. Stir until well blended. Gradually add half-and-half. Cook, stirring constantly, until mixture thickens and comes to boil. Stir in champagne, mushrooms and shrimp. Add honey. Serve over chicken breasts.

Ruth's Chicken and Artichoke Casserole

MAKES 12 SERVINGS

2¼ pounds boneless, skinless chicken breast halves, cubed

Salt and pepper to taste

8 tablespoons butter

½ cup all-purpose flour

3 cups half-and-half

2 (15½-ounce) cans artichoke hearts, drained and chopped

2 pounds mushrooms, sliced, sautéed and drained

1 tablespoon chopped pimiento

1 cup sherry

2 tablespoons Worcestershire sauce

2 teaspoons salt

3 cups cooked wild rice blend

½ cup Parmesan cheese

Season chicken with salt and pepper. Lightly cook chicken, stirring constantly, 3 to 4 minutes in a well-greased skillet over medium heat. Remove from heat. Set aside. In a saucepan, melt butter and whisk in flour. Cook 4 minutes. Add half-and-half. Cook and stir until sauce starts to thicken. Add cooked chicken, artichokes, mushrooms, pimientos, sherry, Worcestershire sauce, salt and wild rice. Place mixture in a 13x9x2 baking dish. Sprinkle with Parmesan cheese. Bake at 350 degrees 25 minutes or until bubbly.

Wok Cashew Chicken

MAKES 4 SERVINGS

1 cup chicken broth

2 tablespoons cornstarch

¼ teaspoon sugar

3 tablespoons vegetable oil

1 cup diced chicken breast, uncooked

½ cup fresh mushrooms, stemmed and sliced

½ cup canned bamboo shoots, drained

½ cup sliced water chestnuts

½ cup snow peas

½ cup cashews, toasted

Soy sauce to taste

Hot cooked rice

Combine broth, cornstarch and sugar and mix well. Set aside. Heat wok and swirl oil around the sides and bottom. Stir-fry chicken until tender. Add mushrooms and cook about 1 minute. Add bamboo shoots and water chestnuts. Cook about 30 seconds. Add snow peas, stir-frying until heated through. Push chicken and vegetables up the sides of the wok. Add broth mixture and stir constantly until sauce thickens. Combine chicken and vegetables into sauce. Add cashews and soy sauce. Mix gently and serve immediately. Serve over rice.

Herb Encrusted Rack of Lamb

MAKES 2 TO 4 SERVINGS

Rack of lamb, rinsed and pat dry	2-3 tablespoons olive oil
⅛ teaspoon salt	1½ cups fresh white bread crumbs
⅛ teaspoon pepper	1 tablespoon butter, melted
⅓ cup Dijon mustard	1 tablespoon chopped parsley
1 tablespoon soy sauce	1 tablespoon dried rosemary
2 garlic cloves, minced	2 teaspoons dried thyme

Season lamb with salt and pepper. Whisk mustard, soy sauce and garlic together in a small bowl. By droplets, add oil, stirring constantly, to make a thick paste. Rub mixture onto lamb. Combine bread crumbs, butter, parsley, rosemary and thyme. Press bread mixture onto mustard coated lamb. Roast at 375 degrees until internal temperature reaches 130 degrees. Let stand 5 minutes before carving.

The FIRST fireproof building in the United States, today a National Historic Landmark and open to the public, was designed by Charleston architect Robert Mills, also known for designing famous public buildings which include the Washington Monument and the Treasury Building in Washington, D.C. The building, designed as a repository for public documents and today home of the archives and collections of the South Carolina Historical Society, was completed in 1827 at the corner of Chalmers and Meeting Streets and cost $56,000.00 to build. Its construction is of simple Greek Doric style, surrounded by four massive columns. The roof is covered with copper, and the window frames and sashes are all of iron with shutters. The interior stone steps rise from the basement to the third floor and are lighted by a skylight in the roof.

Grilled Quail with Shiitake Port Sauce

MAKES 6 SERVINGS

Quail

6   quail, rinsed and flattened

2   cups Italian dressing

Shiitake Port Sauce

½   pound shiitake mushroom caps, sliced

½   teaspoon minced garlic

2   tablespoons unsalted butter

1   cup chicken broth

¼   cup port

2   teaspoons Worcestershire sauce

1   teaspoon balsamic vinegar

Salt and pepper to taste

Quail

Marinate quail in Italian dressing for 2 hours. Grill 3 minutes on each side over high heat. Baste each side with dressing while cooking. Serve with shiitake port sauce.

Shiitake Port Sauce

Sauté shiitake mushrooms and garlic in butter. Add broth, port and Worcestershire sauce. Simmer sauce until reduced to about ¾ cup. Stir in vinegar and season with salt and pepper. Serve with grilled quail.

Glazed Ham

MAKES 25 TO 30 SERVINGS

1 (12 pound) precooked ham	1 tablespoon prepared mustard
1 cup packed light brown sugar	2 tablespoons orange marmalade

Preheat oven to 350 degrees. Remove all but a thin layer of fat from ham. Diagonally score ham, fat side up, at 1 inch intervals. Combine brown sugar, mustard and marmalade. Rub mixture over top and sides of ham. Bake for 80 to 90 minutes.

Scalloped Potatoes and Pork Chops

MAKES 8 SERVINGS

8 (½ inch thick) pork chops	Salt and pepper to taste
4 tablespoons butter	½ cup all-purpose flour
6 Russet potatoes, peeled and sliced ¼ inch thick	1 cup shredded Cheddar cheese
2 medium onions, thinly sliced	2 cups milk

In a skillet, brown chops in butter on each side. Set aside. In a 13x9x2 inch baking dish, layer potatoes and onions. Season with salt and pepper. Sprinkle flour and cheese. Repeat layers. Slowly pour milk over potatoes. Top with pork chops. Bake at 325 degrees about 1 hour.

Pulled Pork BBQ

MAKES 8 TO 10 SERVINGS

Pulled Pork

1   (4 to 5 pound) pork rump roast, salted and peppered

8   tablespoons butter, melted

1   cup red wine vinegar

Salt, pepper and crushed red pepper to taste

Vinegar Base Sauce

8   tablespoons butter

2   cups red wine vinegar

Southern BBQ Sauce

1   medium onion, finely chopped

2   tablespoons butter

1   cup bottled chili sauce

4   tablespoons cider vinegar

2   tablespoons packed brown sugar

4   tablespoons lemon juice

4   tablespoons bottled BBQ sauce

½   teaspoon dry mustard

3   tablespoons Worcestershire sauce

Pulled Pork

Heat charcoal grill and add soaked hickory chips. Grill roast using indirect heat. Combine butter and vinegar and baste roast every 30 minutes. Cook until meat is tender and falling off the bone. Pull pork into small pieces as soon as it is cool enough to handle. Season with salt, pepper and crushed red pepper. We at Hamby Catering serve this with either Vinegar Base Sauce or Southern BBQ Sauce.

Vinegar Base Sauce

Combine butter and vinegar in a small saucepan. Cook over low heat until butter melts. Blend well. Pour over pulled pork to taste.

Southern BBQ Sauce

Sauté onions in butter until tender. Add chili sauce, vinegar, brown sugar, juice, BBQ sauce, mustard and Worcestershire sauce. Simmer over low heat 30 minutes. Pour over pulled pork.

Maple-Mustard Glazed Pork Roast

MAKES 6 SERVINGS

1   (2 to 3 pound) boneless pork
    loin roast
⅔   cup maple-flavored syrup
3   tablespoons Dijon mustard
2   tablespoons cider vinegar
2   tablespoons soy sauce

Salt and pepper to taste
1   pound carrots, peeled and
    quartered
6   medium red potatoes, peeled
    and halved

Place roast in a shallow roasting pan. Combine maple syrup, mustard, vinegar, soy sauce, salt and pepper. Pour syrup mixture evenly over roast. Bake at 350 degrees about 1 hour or until internal temperature reaches 155 to 160 degrees. Add carrots and potatoes during last 30 minutes. Let stand 10 minutes before carving. Slice roast and place on a platter accompanied by vegetables.

Glazed Pork Tenderloin with Artichoke Relish

MAKES 4 TO 6 SERVINGS

¼   cup olive oil
½   cup soy sauce
3   garlic cloves, minced
1   teaspoon ground ginger
2   (12-ounce) whole pork
    tenderloins

¼   cup honey
2   tablespoons packed brown
    sugar
2   teaspoons Dijon mustard
1   teaspoon coarse ground pepper

Combine oil, soy sauce, garlic and ginger. Pour into a zip-top plastic bag over tenderloins. Marinate 2 to 3 hours. Remove pork from marinade and pat dry. Combine honey, brown sugar, mustard and pepper and rub over pork. Place pork in a lightly greased roasting pan. Bake at 350 degrees 20 minutes or until meat thermometer registers 160 degrees. Let stand 10 minutes, slice thinly and serve with artichoke relish (in condiment section of grocery store).

Roast Turkey

MAKES 12 SERVINGS

Turkey

1   (14 pound) fresh turkey
¼   cup vegetable oil

Salt to taste
Coarsely ground black pepper to
    taste

Turkey Broth

Turkey giblets and neck
6-8 cups water

2   ribs celery with leaves
Salt and pepper to taste

Turkey

Remove giblets and neck from turkey. Reserve to make broth. Rinse turkey, inside
and out, with cold water and pat dry. Sprinkle cavity with salt . Brush outside with
oil. Season with salt and coarsely ground pepper. Place turkey, breast-side up, on
a rack in a shallow roasting pan. Bake at 325 degrees until internal temperature
reaches 180 degrees. Let stand 15 minutes before carving. Serve with cornbread
dressing and giblet gravy.

Turkey Broth

Rinse giblets and neck in cold water. Place in a large saucepan. Add water, celery
and season with salt and pepper. Simmer over low-medium heat until reduced by
one-third to one-half. Remove giblets and neck. Strain broth through cheesecloth
or fine mesh sieve. Set aside to make giblet gravy. May be made a day in advance
or several hours before roasting turkey and making dressing.

Cornbread Dressing with Giblet Gravy

MAKES 12 SERVINGS

Cornbread Dressing

4	tablespoons butter or margarine, melted		1	teaspoon poultry seasoning
1½	cups finely chopped celery		3	eggs, beaten
1½	cups chopped onion		4	cups crumbled cornbread
2	teaspoons dried sage or to taste		3	cups herb-seasoned stuffing mix
				Turkey broth to moisten mixture

Giblet Gravy

1	cup pan drippings from turkey		½	teaspoon pepper
¼	cup cornstarch		½-1	teaspoon poultry seasoning
3	cups reserved turkey broth, divided		½	cup chopped turkey neck meat
½	teaspoon salt		½	cup chopped giblets

Cornbread Dressing

Preheat oven to 350 degrees. Melt butter in saucepan. Sauté celery and onions 10 to 12 minutes or until tender. Remove from heat. Stir in sage, poultry seasoning and eggs. Add cornbread and stuffing mix and toss gently to mix. Add broth until mixture is the consistency of raw cornbread. Spread mixture into a greased 13x9x2 inch baking dish. Bake at 350 degrees 45 minutes.

Giblet Gravy

Refrigerate turkey pan drippings. Discard top layer of fat. Combine cornstarch and ½ cup turkey broth in a large saucepan and mix well. Add pan drippings, remaining 2½ cups turkey broth, salt, pepper and poultry seasoning. Bring to boil, stirring constantly. Add turkey and giblets. Boil 1 minute longer, stirring constantly. Serve with dressing. Makes 4 cups.

Low Country Blue Crab Fingers

12-18 live blue crabs   **6   quarts water**
⅓   cup seafood seasoning

Plunge live crabs headfirst into seasoned, boiling water. Cover and return to boiling point. Lower heat and simmer for 15 minutes, or until shells turn red. Drain and rinse the crabs and let them cool enough to handle. Genlty, break the fingers (claws) off where they are attached to the body. Very carefully crack the claws with a nutcracker and remove the shells to expose the meat of the fingers. Serve on a bed of ice with Christen's Mustard Sauce, page 181.

FRAN'S NOTE

Prepared, ready-to-serve Low Country Blue Crab
fingers can be purchased from your local seafood market.

Crab Cakes Imperial

MAKES 8 TO 10 SERVINGS

1   **pound crabmeat, picked
    through**
1   **medium size onion, chopped**
3   **green onions, chopped**
1   **tablespoon chopped pimiento,
    drained**
12 **saltine crackers, crushed**

1   **egg, beaten**
½   **cup mayonnaise**
1   **tablespoon Worcestershire
    sauce**
Salt and pepper to taste
Tabasco sauce to taste

Combine crabmeat, onions, green onions, pimientos, cracker crumbs, egg, mayonnaise, Worcestershire sauce, salt, pepper and Tabasco in a bowl. Gently mix and form into 2 inch patties. Bake at 350 degrees 20 to 25 minutes.

Pecan-Crusted Grouper

MAKES 4 SERVINGS

½ cup cornflake crumbs, crushed
¼ cup finely ground pecans
¼ teaspoon paprika
⅛ teaspoon garlic powder
⅛ teaspoon cayenne pepper

1 pound grouper fillet, cut into
   4 pieces
1 egg white, slightly beaten
2 tablespoons lemon juice
Salt and pepper to taste

Preheat oven to 450 degrees. In large zip-top plastic bag, combine crumbs, pecans, paprika, garlic powder and cayenne. Dip fish pieces into egg white. Add dipped fish to crumb mixture and shake to coat. Place on a greased 15x10x1 inch baking sheet. Bake 15 to 20 minutes or until fish flakes easily with fork. Sprinkle with lemon juice and season with salt and pepper.

Linda's Fried Oysters

MAKES 4 SERVINGS

2 eggs
1 cup milk
1 pint oysters, drained

½ package House Autry seafood
   crumbs
Vegetable oil

In small bowl, beat eggs and add milk. Dip oysters in egg mixture, then roll in crumbs. Heat oil in deep fat fryer to 350 degrees. Drop oysters one at a time into hot oil and cook until golden brown. Drain on wire rack.

Sea Island Crabmeat Remick

MAKES 6 SERVINGS

6   ramekins or crab shells, greased

1   pound lump crabmeat, drained
    and picked through

1   teaspoon dry mustard

½   teaspoon paprika

½   teaspoon celery salt

½   teaspoon Tabasco sauce

½   cup bottled chili sauce

1   teaspoon tarragon vinegar

1½ cups mayonnaise

6   slices bacon, cooked crisp and
    crumbled

Divide crabmeat evenly into 6 ramekins or crab shells. Bake at 350 degrees until thoroughly heated. Combine mustard, paprika, celery salt and Tabasco in a bowl. Add chili sauce and vinegar, stirring well. Whisk in mayonnaise. Spread mixture over crabmeat and place under broiler until bubbly. Top with bacon and serve.

FRAN'S NOTE

This is an entrée I enjoyed at a restaurant in Outer Banks, N.C. With this entrée, they served rice, salad, a medley of mixed vegetables and rolls.

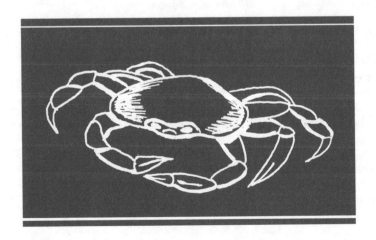

Oyster Pie

MAKES 10 TO 12 SERVINGS

30 saltine crackers, crushed
48 ounces select oysters, drained
1 teaspoon salt, divided
Freshly ground pepper to taste

8 tablespoons butter, sliced and divided
2 cups milk
1 teaspoon Worcestershire sauce
2-3 dashes Tabasco sauce

Layer a third of cracker crumbs into a buttered 3 quart casserole dish. Layer with half oysters. Sprinkle with ½ teaspoon salt and pepper. Dot with half butter slices. Layer a third of crumbs and all of remaining butter slices. Layer remaining oysters. Sprinkle with ½ teaspoon salt and pepper. Spread remaining crumbs on top. Whisk together milk, Worcestershire sauce and Tabasco. Pour over casserole. Bake at 400 degrees 15 to 20 minutes or until thoroughly heated. Do not overcook.

Sautéed Scallops

MAKES 4 SERVINGS

1 tablespoon butter
1 teaspoon olive oil
1 garlic clove
4 tablespoons minced green onion
4 tablespoons minced parsley

1½ pounds large scallops
2 dashes paprika
Generous sprinkling of salt
Fresh ground pepper to taste
1 teaspoon fresh lemon juice
Grated Parmesan cheese (optional)

Melt butter and oil in skillet. Add garlic and sauté over medium-low heat 1 minute. Discard garlic. Add onions and parsley and sauté 3 minutes. Sauté scallops 5 minutes or until done. Add paprika, salt and pepper. Remove scallops with slotted spoon. Arrange on warm plates. Add lemon juice into sauce remaining in skillet. Stir until well blended. Pour over scallops. Top with Parmesan cheese.

Poached Scallops

MAKES 4 SERVINGS

Scallops

2	cups water	½	teaspoon salt
1	cup white wine	2	tablespoons lemon juice
1	lemon, cut in half		Lemon wedges for garnish
1	pound sea scallops		

Horseradish and Lime Sauce

½ cup mayonnaise

1½ teaspoons fresh lime juice

1½ tablespoons bottled horseradish

½ teaspoon fresh grated lime zest

½ teaspoon freshly ground black pepper

1 tablespoon honey

Scallops

Add water, wine and lemon halves to a medium stockpot and bring to simmer. Add scallops. Simmer 2 to 3 minutes until center of scallops are opaque. Remove with slotted spoon. Sprinkle with salt and lemon juice. Spread on baking sheet and place in refrigerator to cool. To serve, place on serving platter. Garnish with lemon wedges and serve with Horseradish and Lime Sauce.

Horseradish and Lime Sauce

Whisk together mayonnaise, juice, horseradish, lime zest, pepper and honey in a bowl. Blend well.

Baked Red Snapper with Crusty Herbs

MAKES 4 SERVINGS

Marinade

¼ cup fresh lemon juice

½ cup dry white wine

¼ cup minced onion

½ cup olive oil

Snapper

4 (6-ounce) red snapper fillets

Salt and pepper to taste

½ pound shrimp, peeled, deveined and cooked

2 tablespoons minced fresh parsley

1 tablespoon capers, drained and finely chopped

¼ teaspoon crushed dried basil

1 cup cracker crumbs

¼ cup mayonnaise

⅓ cup freshly grated Parmesan cheese

Lemon wedges for garnish

Marinade

In a bowl, whisk together lemon juice, wine, onions and oil.

Snapper

In a baking dish combine the fillets with all but ¼ cup of the marinade. Cover and marinate in refrigerator for 3 hours, turning every hour. Remove from marinade and pat dry. Season with salt and pepper. Place in 13x9x2 baking dish. Combine shrimp, parsley, capers, basil, crumbs, mayonnaise, Parmesan cheese and remaining ¼ cup marinade. Bake fillets at 400 degrees 10 minutes on middle rack. Spread shrimp mixture on fillets and bake 5 minutes longer. Broil 5 minutes about 4 inches from heat source or until topping is crisp and golden. Garnish with lemon wedges.

Seafood Soufflé

MAKES 12 SERVINGS

8 slices white bread, divided

1 pound fresh crabmeat, picked through

1½ pounds shrimp, peeled, deveined and lightly sautéed

¾ cup mayonnaise

1 onion, finely chopped

1 bell pepper, chopped

1 cup chopped celery

2 cups whole milk

4 eggs, well beaten

1 teaspoon salt

Pepper to taste

1 (10¾-ounce) can cream of mushroom soup

1 cup shredded Cheddar cheese

Cube 4 bread slices with crusts on and place in a greased 13x9x2 inch baking dish. Combine crabmeat, shrimp, mayonnaise, onions, peppers and celery. Spread mixture over cubed bread. Trim crusts from remaining bread slices and cube it. Place on top of seafood mixture. Whisk together milk, eggs, salt and pepper. Pour over bread. Cover and refrigerate overnight. Remove from refrigerator and allow to warm to room temperature. Spread soup on top and sprinkle with cheese. Bake at 325 degrees 1 hour.

Chicken or Shrimp Supreme

MAKES 8 SERVINGS

4 ounces fresh sliced button mushrooms

2 tablespoons olive oil

3 tablespoons butter

3 tablespoons all-purpose flour

1½ cups half-and-half, warmed

1 tablespoon sliced green onions

2 teaspoons minced parsley

½ teaspoon salt or to taste

1 teaspoon Tabasco sauce

1 tablespoon sherry

3 cups chopped cooked chicken

1½ pounds medium shrimp, peeled, deveined, cooked and coarsely chopped

8 frozen puffed pastry shells, baked

Sauté mushrooms in oil. Set aside. Melt butter over low heat in a saucepan. Whisk in flour. Slowly stir in warmed half-and-half, onions, parsley, salt and Tabasco. Cook and stir until sauce thickens. Remove from heat. Add sherry, chicken or shrimp. Serve hot in puffed pastry shells.

Shrimp Alfredo

MAKES 4 SERVINGS

8 tablespoons butter

2 tablespoons flour

2 tablespoons white wine

1 cup milk

1 cup Parmesan cheese

¼ teaspoon ground nutmeg

¼ teaspoon salt

¼ teaspoon coarsely ground pepper

1 pound shrimp, peeled, deveined and cooked

8 ounces egg noodles, cooked

Melt butter in a skillet over medium-low heat. Whisk in flour until smooth. Cook and stir 4 minutes. Add wine and milk, whisking constantly until smooth. Add cheese, nutmeg, salt and pepper. (Add more milk if the sauce is too thick.) Fold in cooked shrimp. Serve hot over noodles.

Shrimp Curry

MAKES 8 TO 10 SERVINGS

¾ cup chopped onion

¾ cup chopped bell pepper

¾ cup finely chopped celery

8 tablespoons butter, divided

½ cup sifted all-purpose flour

3 cups water or canned chicken broth

1 cup peeled, finely chopped Granny Smith apple

2½ teaspoons curry powder

Dash of cayenne pepper

1 teaspoon minced garlic

1 teaspoon prepared horseradish

1 teaspoon salt

3 pounds shrimp, peeled, deveined and cooked

¾ cup sliced mushrooms, sautéed and reserve drippings

Hot cooked rice

Garnish with any of the following: chutney, chopped salted peanuts, chopped crisp bacon, flaked toasted coconut, raisins, kumquat pickles

Sauté onions, peppers and celery in 2 tablespoons butter until tender. Set aside. Melt 6 tablespoons butter in a saucepan. Whisk in flour to make a paste. Stir in water or broth until well blended. Add onions, peppers, celery, apples, curry, cayenne, garlic, horseradish and salt and blend well. Simmer 20 minutes. Add shrimp and mushrooms with drippings. Simmer 3 minutes longer, stirring constantly. Serve hot over cooked rice and garnish with choice of condiments.

Frogmore Stew

MAKES 10 SERVINGS

¼ cup Old Bay Seasoning

2 tablespoons salt

2 teaspoons pepper

2 medium onions, cut into
    quarters

3 pounds sausage

2 pounds new potatoes

10 ears corn, shucked, silked and
    cut into half

4 pounds shrimp, rinsed

Fill a large stockpot one-third full of water. Add Old Bay seasoning, salt, pepper and onions to water. Bring to boil. Add sausage and cook about 30 minutes until sausage has flavored water. Add potatoes and cook about 10 minutes or until tender. Add corn and cook 8 minutes. Add shrimp and cook 3 to 5 minutes until shrimp turn pink. Drain and serve immediately. Ladle each serving with sausage, potatoes, corn and shrimp. Serve cocktail sauce with shrimp and butter for corn.

Curried Rice and Shrimp

MAKES 12 SERVINGS

¾ cup chopped onion

8 tablespoons margarine

1 tablespoon curry powder or to
    taste

1 teaspoon pepper

2 teaspoons salt

3 cups cooked rice

5 pounds shrimp, peeled,
    deveined and cooked

1 cup chopped pecans

1 cup raisins

12 slices bacon, cooked and
    crumbled

Sauté onions in margarine. Add curry, pepper and salt. Combine onion mixture, rice, shrimp, pecans and raisins. Place mixture in a 13x9x2 inch baking dish. Bake at 350 degrees 20 minutes. Before serving, sprinkle with crumbled bacon.

Shrimp-Fried Rice

MAKES 6 SERVINGS

3 tablespoons vegetable oil	½ pound fresh mushrooms, sliced
3 cups cooked white rice	¼ cup soy sauce
2 eggs, beaten	Dash of white pepper
½ cup chopped green onions, including tops	1 cup fresh shrimp, peeled, deveined, cooked and diced

Heat oil in a large skillet. Sauté rice about 5 minutes. Pour eggs over rice and cook just until eggs are set. Add onions and mushrooms. Stir-fry 1 minute. Add soy sauce, pepper and shrimp and mix well.

Shrimp Scampi

MAKES 8 SERVINGS

1 medium onion, finely chopped	2 pounds large shrimp, peeled and deveined
4 garlic cloves, minced	2 tablespoons grated Parmesan cheese
8 tablespoons butter or margarine, melted	2 tablespoons chopped fresh parsley
2 tablespoons fresh lemon juice	8 ounces cooked fettuccine or 6 cups cooked rice
½ teaspoon steak sauce	
½ teaspoon Worcestershire sauce	
1 teaspoon Tabasco sauce	

In a large skillet, sauté onions and garlic in butter for 3 to 4 minutes over medium heat, stirring constantly. Add juice, steak sauce, Worcestershire sauce and Tabasco. Bring to boil. Add shrimp and cook 5 minutes, stirring constantly, or until shrimp turns pink. Add Parmesan cheese and sprinkle with parsley. Serve over fettuccine or rice.

 **VEGETABLES, RICE**
AND
ACCOMPANIMENTS

Looking over the Marsh Where Rice was Grown

If buried sounds could come alive
in sunrise, from the Carolina Marsh,
along the river where I live, you'd hear
a fleet of fatigued feet sink rice into thick
mush, like an automated machine
driven by the rhythm of West African
songs, stitching bondsmen in a shroud
of despair. And in harvest's

heat, if buried sights could come alive
you'd see a force, thinned by hard labor
and epidemics carried away in wooden
carts, leaving only the hearty-weak
to beat and husk grain, an exchange for
a town shaped by "Carolina Gold."

And yet, at dark, you'd hear prayers rise
from rows of huts...by those stored
overnight, stacked, like precious tools.

~ *Elizabeth Bullock Godfrey*

A Portrait of Elegance

The I. Jenkins Mikell Town House on Rutledge Ave. was built around 1853 and reflects the grandeur of the Antebellum South, and the owner's wealth from Sea Island cotton. My elementary class from James Simons school took a field trip to this home after it had been adapted for use as the County Library. We were escorted from the marble entrance, through part of the elegant house to the room that contained the children's collection of neatly stacked books. The librarian, a petite lady with a welcoming smile, greeted us and read a story to the class. I can't recall the story, but I remember being absolutely, fascinated with the magnificent portico that was embellished with tall Corinthian columns facing the garden to the south. Magnolias, palmettos and other greenery framed this portrait of enduring elegance.

~ *Elizabeth Bullock Godfrey*

Artichoke Bottoms Stuffed with Spinach

MAKES 25 OR MORE ARTICHOKES

2 (10-ounce) packages frozen
chopped spinach, thawed

½ cup minced onion

6 tablespoons butter

½ cup sour cream

¾ cup Parmesan cheese, divided

½ teaspoon salt

¼ teaspoon pepper

Dash of cayenne pepper

3 (14-ounce) cans artichoke
bottoms, drained

Cook spinach according to the package directions and drain. Sauté onions in butter until tender. Stir in spinach, sour cream, ½ cup Parmesan cheese, salt, pepper and cayenne. Spoon mixture onto artichoke bottoms. Place in a greased shallow baking dish. Sprinkle with ¼ cup Parmesan cheese. Bake at 350 degrees 20 minutes.

Asparagus Spears with Lemon Butter

MAKES 8 SERVINGS

2 pounds fresh asparagus, ends
trimmed

2 tablespoons butter or
margarine

¼ cup lemon juice

½ teaspoon salt

⅛ teaspoon pepper

Freshly grated Parmesan cheese

Blanch asparagus in boiling water for 5 minutes until crisp-tender. Drain and plunge in ice water to stop cooking. Drain again. Melt butter in a skillet over medium heat. Stir in lemon juice. Place asparagus in a single layer on a serving platter. Sprinkle with salt and pepper and drizzle with butter sauce. Repeat with remaining asparagus. Top with Parmesan cheese.

Green Beans with Sautéed Slivered Almonds

MAKES 4 SERVINGS

½ pound fresh green beans,
sliced into 1-inch pieces

½ cup blanched slivered almonds

2 tablespoons butter, divided

2 teaspoons vegetable oil

1 teaspoon chopped fresh sage
or ¼ teaspoon dried

¼ teaspoon salt

¼ cup dry sherry

Blanch beans in salted, boiling water and cook until crisp-tender. Drain and immerse in cold water. Drain again. Sauté beans and almonds in 1 tablespoon butter mixed with oil for 3 to 5 minutes until almonds are golden. Stir in sage and salt. Remove to a warm plate. Add sherry to skillet. Cook over high heat to a reduced syrupy consistency. Stir in remaining 1 tablespoon butter. Drizzle over beans and almonds. Serve immediately.

Marinated Green Beans or Asparagus

MAKES 4 TO 6 SERVINGS

1½ cups white vinegar

1 cup water

¾ cup sugar

2 teaspoons salt

10 whole cloves

2 cinnamon sticks

2 tablespoons chopped fresh dill
(optional)

1 pound fresh green beans, ends
trimmed or fresh asparagus
spears

Combine vinegar, water, sugar, salt, cloves, cinnamon sticks and dill and mix well. Set aside. Blanch beans or asparagus in boiling water until crisp-tender. Drain and immediately plunge into ice water. Drain again. Pour marinade over beans or asparagus. Marinate beans for 4 hours and asparagus for only 30 minutes prior to serving. Asparagus will turn brown with longer marinating.

Tangy Green Beans with Pimiento

MAKES 6 SERVINGS

1½ pounds fresh green beans, trimmed

4   slices bacon

1   large white onion, chopped

3   garlic cloves, minced

1   (4-ounce) jar diced pimiento, drained

¼   cup red wine vinegar

1   teaspoon sugar

½   teaspoon salt

½   teaspoon pepper

½   teaspoon cumin seeds

Blanch beans in boiling water for 4 to 5 minutes. Drain and plunge into ice water to stop the cooking. Drain and set aside. Cook bacon in a large skillet until crisp and drain on paper towels, reserving 2 tablespoons drippings. Crumble bacon and set aside. Sauté onions and garlic in drippings over medium-high heat until tender. Stir in pimiento, vinegar, sugar, salt, pepper and cumin seeds. Stir in beans and reduce heat. Cover and simmer for 5 minutes. Sprinkle with bacon and serve.

Zesty Broccoli Spears

MAKES 4 SERVINGS

1   pound fresh broccoli, rinsed

4   tablespoons olive oil

2   tablespoons fresh lemon juice

1   garlic clove, minced

¼   teaspoon salt

Dash of pepper

Cut broccoli into serving-size spears. Steam for 5 minutes until crisp-tender. Combine oil, juice, garlic, salt and pepper. Drizzle over broccoli.

Orange-Glazed Carrots

MAKES 8 SERVINGS

4	tablespoons butter	1	cup orange marmalade
¼	cup chicken broth		Freshly ground pepper to taste
¼	teaspoon salt	2	tablespoons Grand Marnier, if desired
2	pounds fresh baby carrots, trimmed	2	tablespoons chopped parsley

Combine butter, broth and salt in a heavy saucepan. Bring to boil. Add the carrots and cook covered over medium heat until barely tender. Uncover and stir in the marmalade. Cook, stirring constantly, over low heat until liquid has reduced to a glaze. Season with additional salt and pepper. Add Grand Marnier. May be refrigerated overnight. Before serving, reheat gently, stirring carrots until heated through. Garnish with chopped parsley.

Maybell's Collard Greens

MAKES 12 SERVINGS

3	large bunches collard greens, rinse well in cold water, drain and remove stems	3	teaspoons salt
		1	teaspoon pepper
2	pounds smoked ham hocks	1	teaspoon sugar

Cut greens into small pieces. Set aside. Cook ham hocks in boiling water until the meat falls off the bones. Remove all fat and bones, reserving meat and strained broth. Add greens to broth and cook, covered, over low heat for 1 hour or until greens are tender. Add reserved meat, salt, pepper and sugar. Simmer 15 minutes longer.

Duchess Potatoes

MAKES 16 SERVINGS

4 pounds potatoes, peeled and cooked
½ cup milk
12 tablespoons butter, softened
½ teaspoon salt
¼ teaspoon pepper
4 eggs, beaten
8 tablespoons butter, melted
½ cup grated Parmesan cheese

Combine cooked potatoes with milk, butter, salt, pepper and eggs. Beat with an electric mixer until smooth. Using a pastry bag, pipe individual potato portions onto a greased parchment paper-lined baking sheet. Brush with melted butter and sprinkle Parmesan cheese. Bake at 425 degrees 15 minutes or until browned.

Spinach Rockefeller

MAKES 6 SERVINGS

4 tablespoons butter, divided
½ cup finely chopped onion
3 (10-ounce) packages frozen chopped spinach, cooked and drained
¾ teaspoon thyme
1 teaspoon salt
½ cup seasoned bread crumbs
3 eggs, slightly beaten
½ cup grated Parmesan cheese

Melt 3 tablespoons butter in a large saucepan. Sauté onions until tender. Add spinach, thyme, salt and bread crumbs and mix well. Add eggs and heat, stirring constantly, until well blended. Place in a 1 quart casserole dish. Sprinkle with cheese and dot with remaining 1 tablespoon butter. Bake at 350 degrees 15 minutes or until brown and thoroughly heated.

Squash Casserole

MAKES 4 SERVINGS

1 pound yellow squash	½ cup onions
4 tablespoons butter, melted	¾ cup shredded sharp Cheddar cheese
2 eggs	
1 tablespoon all-purpose flour	2 cups buttery cracker crumbs, if desired
½ teaspoon salt or to taste	
⅛ teaspoon pepper	

Cook squash in a small amount of salted boiling water until tender. Drain well and chop. Combine butter, eggs, flour, salt, pepper, onions and cheese and mix well. Stir in squash. Spoon mixture into a lightly greased 1 quart casserole dish. Top evenly with cracker crumbs. Bake at 350 degrees 30 minutes or until set.

Sweet Potato Soufflé

MAKES 6 SERVINGS

3 cups hot mashed sweet potatoes	½ teaspoon vanilla
	½ cup milk
½ cup sugar	½ cup packed light brown sugar
½ teaspoon salt	⅓ cup all-purpose flour
2 large eggs	1 cup chopped pecans
7 tablespoons butter, softened, divided	

In large bowl, combine sweet potatoes, sugar, salt, eggs, 4 tablespoons butter, vanilla and milk. Pour mixture into a greased 1½ quart casserole dish. Combine brown sugar, flour, pecans and remaining 3 tablespoons butter in a small bowl. Top sweet potato mixture with crumbled mixture. Bake at 350 degrees 35 minutes.

Tomato Pie

MAKES 8 SERVINGS

1 (9-inch) deep dish pie crust, baked

3 large tomatoes, peeled, thickly sliced

Salt and pepper to taste

½ cup sliced green onions

½ cup chopped bell pepper

½ cup chopped celery

2 tablespoons vegetable oil

1 cup mayonnaise

1 cup shredded Cheddar cheese

Fresh basil leaves

Place sliced tomatoes on bottom of baked pie crust. Season with salt and pepper. Sauté onions, peppers and celery in oil. Layer over tomatoes. Combine mayonnaise and cheese. Spread over vegetables. Bake at 350 degrees 30 minutes. Remove from oven and sprinkle with basil leaves.

FRAN'S NOTE

Kitchen shears are a handy tool to have in the kitchen. Use them to snip fresh parsley, basil and other fresh herbs. They can also be used to trim pie crust and to cut up candied fruit for fruit cake. Remember to dip shears in hot water occasionally when cutting sticky food.

Oven-Roasted Vegetables

MAKES 6 TO 8 SERVINGS

1 medium zucchini squash, cut into bite-size pieces

1 medium yellow squash, cut into bite-size pieces

1 medium sweet red pepper, cut into bite-size pieces

1 medium yellow pepper, cut into bite-size pieces

1 pound fresh asparagus, cut into bite-size pieces

2 portabello mushrooms, cut into strips

1 large onion, cut into bite-size pieces

3 tablespoons extra-virgin olive oil

½ teaspoon salt

½ teaspoon freshly ground pepper

Preheat oven to 450 degrees. Place zucchini, squash, peppers, asparagus, mushrooms and onions in a large roasting pan. Toss with oil, salt and pepper until well coated. Spread in a single layer in the pan. Roast 30 minutes, stirring occasionally, until vegetables are lightly brown and tender.

The FIRST settlers brought cotton seed with them in 1670…and although the crop did not become a major agricultural item at first, American's first cotton export—seven bags valued at about $825.—left Charleston for England in 1748. Following the American Revolution, when indigo was discontinued as an export, cotton took its place, and became the basis for a new facet of plantation culture that soon rivalled the rice society. Sea Island cotton continued to be an important crop until World War I, when the boll weevil put an end to most of the production of the long staple fiber.

Vegetable Casserole

MAKES 8 TO 10 SERVINGS

1	(11-ounce) can white shoe peg corn, drained	½	cup shredded sharp Cheddar cheese
1	(14½-ounce) can French style green beans, drained	1	(10¾-ounce) can cream of celery soup
½	cup chopped celery		Salt and pepper to taste
½	cup chopped onion	2	cups buttery cheese crackers, crushed
¼	cup chopped bell pepper		
½	cup sour cream	4	tablespoons butter, melted
		½	cup slivered almonds

Mix together corn, beans, celery, onions, peppers, sour cream, cheese, soup, salt and pepper. Pour mixture into a 13x9x2 inch baking dish. Combine cracker crumbs with butter and sprinkle over vegetables. Top with slivered almonds. Bake at 350 degrees 45 minutes.

Penne Pasta with Pepperoni and Sun-Dried Tomatoes

MAKES 6 TO 8 SERVINGS

1	cup sun-dried tomatoes in oil	¼	cup chopped fresh parsley
½	cup crumbled blue cheese	1	teaspoon dried oregano
¼	cup shredded Parmesan cheese	¼	cup red wine vinegar
1	teaspoon dried basil	½	cup olive oil
1	(4-ounce) package sliced pepperoni		Salt and pepper to taste
		1	pound penne pasta, cooked

Combine tomatoes, blue cheese, Parmesan cheese, basil, pepperoni, parsley, oregano, vinegar and oil and mix well. Season with salt and pepper. Cook pasta according to package directions. Drain and toss with tomato mixture. Serve hot.

Blake's Favorite Macaroni and Cheese

MAKES 6 SERVINGS

2	cups uncooked macaroni	1	tablespoon flour
2	tablespoons butter	1	teaspoon dry mustard
3	eggs, beaten		Salt and pepper to taste
3	cups milk	½	pound sharp Cheddar cheese, cut in slices

Cook macaroni according to package directions. Drain and add butter. Set aside. Combine eggs, milk, flour, mustard, salt and pepper in a large bowl. Layer macaroni and cheese in a 2 quart casserole dish. Pour egg mixture over top. Bake at 325 degrees 30 minutes or until set.

FRAN'S NOTE

This is my grandson, Blake's, favorite dish. We usually double this recipe and bake in a greased 13x9x2 inch baking dish. Makes a generous portion for a hungry teenager and is great when served for leftovers.

Italian Pasta

MAKES 6 TO 8 SERVINGS

1	cup olive oil	3	garlic cloves, diced
1	teaspoon dried basil	3	Roma tomatoes, sliced
1	teaspoon dried oregano	½	cup grated Romano cheese
1	teaspoon salt	1	pound bow tie pasta
1	teaspoon pepper		

Combine oil, basil, oregano, salt, pepper, garlic, tomatoes and cheese in large bowl. Cook pasta according to package directions. Drain and add to oil mixture. Toss and serve either warm or cold.

FRAN'S NOTE

Perfectly cooked pasta is moist, tender and just slightly resistant to the bite. For best results, pasta must be added to boiling water. For each pound of pasta, bring 5 quarts of water to a rolling boil in a large pot. Add salt and then the pasta gradually so that the water returns to a boil quickly. Stir briefly to separate the pasta.

Easy Curried Rice

MAKES 4 SERVINGS

1½	cups of chicken broth, if using canned, add 4 tablespoons butter and salt to taste	1	cup long grain rice
		½	cup raisins
2	teaspoons curry powder	⅓	cup chopped cashew nuts

In a medium saucepan, bring broth to boil. Add curry and rice. Cover and cook over low heat 20 minutes. Add raisins and nuts.

Caribbean Rice

MAKES 12 SERVINGS

6 cups cooked rice

1½ cups crushed pineapple, drained well

1 cup canned Mandarin oranges, sections cut in half

1 cup diced red sweet pepper

½ cup sliced green onions with tops

½ cup mango chutney

1 teaspoon curry powder

½ teaspoon ground ginger

1 teaspoon almond extract

½ cup slivered almonds, toasted

Combine cooked rice with pineapple, oranges, peppers, onions, chutney, curry, ginger, almond extract and almonds in a large saucepan. Heat over low heat until thoroughly warmed. Serve immediately.

Charleston Red Rice

MAKES 8 SERVINGS

8-10 slices bacon

2 cups chopped onions

½ stalk celery, chopped

½ bell pepper, chopped

1 teaspoon salt

½ teaspoon pepper

3 cups canned diced tomatoes, undrained

½ teaspoon Tabasco sauce

¼ teaspoon curry powder

⅛ teaspoon sugar

4 tablespoons butter, melted

2 cups white rice

1 pound kielbasa sausage, thinly sliced

Cook bacon over medium heat in a large skillet. Crumble bacon and set aside. Sauté onions, celery and peppers in bacon drippings. Stir in salt, pepper, tomatoes, Tabasco, curry and sugar. Mix together butter and rice until well coated. Add tomato mixture and sausage to rice and mix well. Pour mixture into 13x9x2 inch baking dish. Cover and bake at 350 degrees 25 minutes. Top with crumbled bacon before serving.

Exotic Spiced Rice

MAKES 12 SERVINGS

2	cups chopped onion	1½	cups slivered almonds, toasted
¼	cup olive oil	½	cup golden raisins
4	garlic cloves, minced	1	tablespoon lemon zest
1	teaspoon curry powder	½	teaspoon cinnamon
6	cups cooked rice	½	teaspoon salt
1	cup chopped whole dates	½	teaspoon pepper

Sauté onions in oil in a saucepan until translucent. Add garlic and curry. Sauté 1 minute longer. Combine with rice, dates, almonds, raisins, zest, cinnamon, salt and pepper in a glass microwave-safe dish. Heat thoroughly in microwave.

— FRAN'S NOTE —

A good complement for flank steak.

Jenkins Orphanage

When we heard the sounds of cymbals, horns and drums coming from the street, we knew the Jenkins Orphanage Band had arrived. They came into town in an open truck, jumped out with their instruments and after playing a few songs, they scattered around the crowd that gathered and took an offering to help with the expenses of the orphanage.

Brenda's Nice Rice

MAKES 5 SERVINGS

4	tablespoons butter	½	cup white wine
2	small onions, chopped	8	fresh medium-sized mushrooms, sliced
1	cup white or brown rice		
1	large garlic clove, crushed	1	tablespoon chopped pimiento
1	cup chicken broth	1	teaspoon seasoning salt

Melt butter in a large saucepan. Sauté onions until tender. Add rice and cook 5 minutes longer. Stir in garlic, broth, wine, mushrooms, pimientos and salt. Pour mixture into a 2 quart casserole dish. Cover and bake at 350 degrees 30 to 40 minutes.

── FRAN'S NOTE ──

1 cup of raw rice equals 3 cups of cooked rice. Brown rice contains twice as much fiber as white rice and, because of the enrichment it contains, almost three times the amount of iron. Wild rice is richer in protein and vitamins, higher in fiber and lower in calories than either white or brown rice. All rice is sodium free unless salt is added during cooking.

Hoppin' John

MAKES 6 SERVINGS

1 cup dried peas, such as cow peas or black-eyed peas	1 smoked ham hock
5-6 cups water	1 medium onion, chopped
1 dried hot chile pepper (optional)	1 cup long grain white rice

Wash and sort peas. Place them in a large saucepan with water. Discard any peas that float. Add pepper, ham hock and onions. Gently boil 1 hour, 30 minutes until tender, but not mushy or until 2 cups of liquid remains. Add rice. Cover and simmer over low heat 20 minutes, never lifting the lid. Remove from heat and let stand 10 minutes longer. Uncover, fluff with a fork and serve immediately.

Okra and Tomato Pilaf

MAKES 6 SERVINGS

4 slices bacon	2 cups whole tomatoes, drained and chopped
½ cup chopped onion	
4 cups water	4 cups sliced okra
2 cups rice	1 teaspoon salt or to taste
	½ teaspoon pepper

Cook bacon until crisp. Transfer to a paper towel to drain. Crumble bacon and set aside. Sauté onions in bacon drippings until tender. Combine onions with water, rice, tomatoes, okra, salt and pepper. Pour mixture into a 13x9x2 inch baking dish. Cover and bake at 350 degrees 20 minutes or until rice is tender. Top with bacon prior to serving.

Rice Pilaf

MAKES 6 SERVINGS

1 cup uncooked white rice	1 (4-ounce) can of mushroom
1 medium onion, chopped	stems and pieces, undrained
1 cup chopped celery	1 (4-ounce) jar of diced pimiento,
5⅓ tablespoons butter	undrained
1 (10¾-ounce) can chicken broth	2 tablespoons of grated Parmesan
	cheese

Sauté rice, onions and celery in butter. Remove from heat. Stir in broth, mushrooms and pimientos. Pour mixture into 2 quart casserole dish. Cover tightly and bake at 350 degrees 25 minutes or until liquid is absorbed. Sprinkle with Parmesan cheese before serving.

—— FRAN'S NOTE ——

Have you tried the Carolina Gold Rice? It is very good
and it can be purchased now, as it is being grown and harvested locally
in somewhat limited quantities. It is a bit pricey but has been started
from seeds, the variety grown here when we were a colony.

Wild Rice with Dried Cranberries

MAKES 6 SERVINGS

2	cups wild rice	4	tablespoons butter
8	cups water	3	teaspoons chicken base
Pepper to taste		½	cup dried cranberries

Rinse wild rice thoroughly in cold water and drain. In large saucepan, bring water to rapid boil. Add rice. Cover and cook for 45 minutes or until rice is chewy but tender. Remove rice from saucepan and drain. Season with pepper. In a small saucepan, melt butter and mix with chicken base. Stir into rice. While rice is hot, add cranberries.

Fruited Wild Rice Pilaf with Pine Nuts

MAKES 6 SERVINGS

4	cups chicken broth	Zest of 1 orange
1	cup wild rice	Juice of 1 orange
¾	cup dried cranberries	½ cup pine nuts, toasted
1	tablespoon butter	Salt and pepper to taste

Bring broth and wild rice to boil. Reduce heat, cover and simmer 45 minutes or until rice is tender. Add cranberries and cook 5 minutes longer. Drain. Stir in butter, zest, juice, pine nuts and season with salt and pepper.

Zesty Blue Cheese Dressing

MAKES 2 ½ CUPS

¾ cup sour cream
½ teaspoon dry mustard
½ teaspoon pepper
½ teaspoon salt
⅓ teaspoon garlic powder

1 teaspoon Worcestershire sauce
1⅓ cups mayonnaise
1 (4-ounce) package crumbled
   blue cheese

Place sour cream, mustard, pepper, salt, garlic powder, Worcestershire sauce and mayonnaise in a mixing bowl. Blend together by hand. Crumble blue cheese into very small pieces and add. Blend well by hand. Refrigerate for 24 hours prior to using.

Lemon Dill Sauce

MAKES 1 ½ CUPS

¾ cup mayonnaise
¼ cup buttermilk
¼ cup sour cream
2 tablespoons chopped fresh dill

1 tablespoon minced fresh parsley
2 teaspoons fresh lemon juice
1 tablespoon lemon zest
1 garlic clove, crushed

Combine mayonnaise, buttermilk, sour cream, dill, parsley, juice, zest and garlic and mix well. Cover and refrigerate until mixture thickens.

── FRAN'S NOTE ──

Lemon dill sauce is excellent with asparagus.

Cranberry-Orange Relish

MAKES 4 CUPS

4 cups fresh cranberries

2 oranges, unpeeled, seeded and quartered

1 (8-ounce) can crushed pineapple, drained

2 cups sugar

¼ teaspoon salt

In a food processor, coarsely chop cranberries and oranges. Transfer to a bowl. Add pineapple, sugar and salt and mix well. Cover and refrigerate 1 to 2 days before serving.

Rémoulade Sauce

MAKES ABOUT 1 CUP

1 large garlic clove, crushed

1 shallot, finely chopped

2 tablespoons finely chopped fresh parsley

1 anchovy, chopped

2 teaspoons capers

1 teaspoon tomato paste

½ cup mayonnaise

Juice of 1 lemon

¼ teaspoon cayenne pepper

White pepper to taste

Place garlic, shallot, parsley, anchovy, capers, tomato paste, mayonnaise, juice, cayenne and white pepper in a blender. Process until well blended. Refrigerate until ready to use.

Christen's Mustard Sauce

MAKES 1 ½ CUPS

1 cup mayonnaise

1 ½ tablespoons dry mustard

Honey to taste

1 tablespoon steak sauce

1 tablespoon heavy cream or milk

Poppy seeds

Dash of grainy mustard

Blend together mayonnaise, dry mustard, honey, steak sauce, milk, poppy seeds and grainy mustard in a bowl. Refrigerate until needed.

Fresh Tomato Salsa

MAKES 6 CUPS

3 cups fresh Roma tomatoes, seeded and diced

⅔ cup finely diced red onion

⅓ cup chopped green onion

½ cup canned whole kernel corn, drained

½ cup canned black beans, rinsed and pat dry

2 tablespoons chopped fresh cilantro

2 tablespoons sugar

⅓ cup fresh lime juice

2 jalapeño peppers, seeded and finely diced

Mix together tomatoes, onions, corn, beans, cilantro, sugar, juice and peppers in a medium bowl. Refrigerate until thoroughly chilled.

Boiled Peanuts

MAKES 5 POUNDS

5   **pounds fresh raw peanuts**   ⅓ **box of salt**

Place peanuts in a large stockpot and cover completely with water. Add salt and boil peanuts for 1 hour, 30 minutes or until tender. Test for salty taste. If they are salty enough, drain immediately. If peanuts are not salty, soak in salty water until desired taste is reached.

— FRAN'S NOTE —

This is certainly a southern dish that is very popular in the South, but once you developed a taste for boiled peanuts, you are hooked.

FIRST woman artist in America was Henrietta Johnson, who worked in Charleston between 1707 and 1720. Her subjects were mostly women of South Carolina, but her work is a likeness of Robert Johnston, Governor-general of His Majesty's Province of Carolina.

 **DESSERTS**

This is a version of Henry Beckroges' recipe for Vanilla Cakes, which were in great demand during his day, and still remembered by many who had the good fortune to have sampled the cakes. People are still asking if anyone has the recipe for the renowned Vanilla Cakes. As was the custom in those days, recipes were not in writing, but in the head of the baker. Thus, this one has been devised from any and everyone that could remember a tidbit or even guess what may have been in the cake mixture. Hamby Catering has made samples over and over and this version comes closest to the original.

Henry Beckroge, the owner of Beckroge Bakery, retired and closed the door to the bakery in June 1973; thus, causing a stir in the community in search for the Vanilla Cakes. The Post and Courier News people can attest to this, as many written requests have come to them inquiring as to the name and recipe for the cakes. Henry Beckroge undoubtedly left a legacy for his baking, but the zenith, perhaps, is Vanilla Cakes. Elizabeth Bullock Godfrey, a niece of Henry Beckroge and a very close friend to Fran, has contributed to Hamby Catering in so many ways. She was the sampler and taster in devising Hamby's rendition of Vanilla Cakes.

As a historical fact, it is well to remember that the original method of baking required the batter to be dropped on a large sheet of brown paper for baking and when cool, the baked circles were uniformly cut with a metal cutter (biscuit size) before filling with jelly and then the icing. Because the original method was quite labor intensive, we have engaged shortcuts in making the Vanilla Cakes.

Beckroges Vanilla Cakes

3 eggs, separated
3 tablespoons cold water
1 cup sugar, divided

1 cup self-rising flour,
sifted 3 times
1 teaspoon vanilla

Mix egg yolks, water and ½ cup sugar. Beat until lemon colored. Add flour. Beat egg whites, vanilla and ½ cup sugar to form soft peaks. Fold into flour mixture. Put in 2 (9-inch) cake pans. Preheat oven to 425 degrees; put pans in oven and bake for 12 minutes. Remove from oven and place on a rack. When cool, slice layers in half, horizontally, and fill with seedless raspberry jelly, or spread with a mixture of ½ raspberry spread and ½ red currant jelly. Cover with a vanilla icing.

Candlelight Celebrations

My paternal grandparents retired and moved to Summerville, which was considered Charleston's suburb in the pines. Located about twenty-five miles inland, we visited there often. I remember one Christmas Eve (before electricity was brought to their rural area) when we had an awesome event. A pine tree was cut and decorated with small candles clipped to the branches, and lit by our parents and grandparents. Then, they stood around the tree with buckets of water - just in case a fire started - while we basked in the glow of this light in anticipation of the next day's celebration.

In contrast to this, another one of the highlights of our Christmas celebration in the city of Charleston was the Candlelight Service at St. Matthew's Lutheran Church. One of these special services for us occurred in the 1930's. Inside, the Gothic church was decorated with a huge lighted tree, fresh greenery and numerous red poinsettias. Outside, lights illuminated the stained glass windows, so that even in the darkness, we were able to see the rich reds and blues of those windows as we sat in this church.

My three brothers and I sang in the choir and carried lighted candles during the processional. Our youngest brother, Richard, age five, sang a solo, Silent Night, and after the recessional, the entire choir received a "Whitman's Sampler." What a treat!

~ *Elizabeth Bullock Godfrey*

Lib's Apple Crisp

MAKES 6 TO 8 SERVINGS

4 cups sliced apples, peeled and
   cut into ¼ inch slices

1 teaspoon cinnamon

½ cup water

1 cup sugar

¾ cup all-purpose flour

8 tablespoons butter or
   margarine, softened

Whipped cream

Arrange apple slices in buttered baking dish. Add cinnamon and water. Mix together sugar, flour, and butter until crumbly. Spoon over apples and bake, uncovered, at 350 degrees about 40 minutes. Serve hot with whipped cream.

── FRAN'S NOTE ──

1 cup of heavy cream yields 2 cups of whipped cream. When whipping cream, have the cream and all equipment well chilled. Do not sweeten cream until it is partially whipped. Sugar, added too early, will make whipping difficult. Powdered sugar is better than granulated sugar for stability. Do not over-whip the cream or it will turn into butter. Half-and-half and light cream will not whip. Use only whipping cream or heavy cream. The higher the fat content in the cream, the thicker the whipped cream will be.

Austin's Favorite Cake

MAKES 8 TO 1O SERVINGS

1   (18-ounce) package butter
      cake mix
1   cup sour cream
¼   cup sugar

¼   cup water
4   eggs
½   cup vegetable oil

Combine cake mix, sour cream, sugar, water, eggs and oil in a large mixing bowl. Beat on high 4 minutes. Grease three 9 inch round cake pans. Divide batter evenly among pans. Bake at 300 degrees 40 minutes or until cake tester comes out clean. Cool 10 minutes in pan. Cool completely on wire rack. Frost with favorite icing.

— FRAN'S NOTE —

Austin is my grandchild who likes to cook. He sometimes calls to ask directions for a favorite recipe. This recipe is one for him - it's fast, easy and, when paired with chocolate icing, awesome!

Deb's Fresh Apple Cake

MAKES 8 TO 10 SERVINGS

Cake

2 cups sugar

½ cup vegetable oil

2 eggs

2 cups all-purpose flour

2 teaspoons baking soda

2 teaspoons cinnamon

4 cups diced Granny Smith apples

1 teaspoon vanilla

1 cup chopped walnuts

Cream Cheese Frosting

6 tablespoons butter, softened

1 (8-ounce) package cream cheese, softened

1½ teaspoons vanilla

1½ cups powdered sugar

Cake

Beat sugar and oil together with an electric mixer. Add eggs and mix well. In a separate bowl, combine flour, baking soda and cinnamon. Slowly add to creamed mixture. Stir in apples, vanilla and nuts. Divide batter into two greased and floured 9 inch round cake pans. Bake at 325 degrees 30 to 40 minutes. Cool 10 minutes in pan. Invert cooled cake onto a cake plate and frost.

Cream Cheese Frosting

Cream butter, cream cheese and vanilla. Slowly mix in sugar until smooth.

Chocolate Brownie Cakes

MAKES 24 CAKE SQUARES

Cake

2	cups sugar	½	cup vegetable oil
2	cups all-purpose flour	4	tablespoons cocoa
1	teaspoon baking soda	½	cup buttermilk
1	teaspoon cinnamon	2	eggs, slightly beaten
1	cup water	1	teaspoon vanilla
8	tablespoons margarine		

Chocolate Icing

8	tablespoons margarine	1	(16-ounce) box powdered sugar, sifted
4	tablespoons cocoa	1	teaspoon vanilla
6	tablespoons milk	1	cup chopped pecans

Cake

Sift together sugar, flour, baking soda and cinnamon. Set aside. Combine water, margarine, oil and cocoa in a saucepan. Bring to boil. Cool to room temperature and stir into dry ingredients. Set aside. Mix together buttermilk, eggs and vanilla. Stir into chocolate batter. Pour batter into a greased 13x9x2 inch baking dish. Bake at 400 degrees 20 to 25 minutes. Start preparing icing 5 minutes before cake is done and frost cake in pan while hot. Cool and cut into squares.

Chocolate Icing

Combine margarine, cocoa and milk in a saucepan. Bring to boil, being careful not to let it scorch. Slowly add powdered sugar, blending well until smooth. Remove from heat. Add vanilla and nuts.

Charleston Cake Lady's Southern Lady Cake

MAKES 16 TO 18 SERVINGS

1	(18-ounce) package orange supreme cake mix	4	large eggs
⅓	cup sugar	1	teaspoon vanilla
⅔	cup vegetable oil	1	(11-ounce) can Mandarin oranges, undrained

Combine cake mix and sugar together. Add oil, eggs and vanilla and beat until well blended. Beat 4 minutes on medium high. Turn off mixer and add oranges. Beat on low speed until oranges are evenly distributed. Pour batter into a well greased Bundt pan. Bake at 350 degrees 40 minutes or until cake tester comes out clean. If more baking time is needed, check for doneness in increments. Cool cake in the pan.

FRAN'S NOTE

Teresa Pregnall, the Charleston Cake Lady, has added tremendously to Charleston's fame by writing two cookbooks, *Treasured Recipes From the Charleston Cake Lady* and *Special Recipes From the Charleston Cake Lady*. The Hambys are very fortunate and, indeed, deeply grateful for Teresa's graciousness in providing this not yet published recipe for inclusion in this book.

Aunt Julie's White Fruit Cake

MAKES 15 TO 20 SERVINGS

3 cups all-purpose flour	2 teaspoons vanilla
2 teaspoons baking powder	1 cup grated coconut
¾ teaspoon salt	1 pound candied cherries, cut in half
16 tablespoons butter	
2 cups sugar	½ pound pineapple
6 eggs	½ pound citron
1 cup orange juice	1 pound golden raisins
2 teaspoons lemon extract	4 cups pecans

Sift together flour, baking powder and salt three times. Set aside. In a mixing bowl, cream butter and sugar. Add eggs, one at a time, beating well after each addition. Add orange juice, lemon extract and vanilla. Gradually add flour mixture. Fold in coconut, cherries, pineapple, citron, raisins and nuts. Press into a well-greased Bundt pan. Bake at 250 degrees about 3 hours.

FRAN'S NOTE

For many years women in my family have traditionally filled their homes with fragrant smells of holiday baking, especially those of their favorite Christmas cakes. Of course, each cake is made from scratch. To bake a perfect cake, it is necessary to observe a few rules of fine baking. Read the recipe, thoroughly, before you begin to make it. Have all the ingredients at hand and at room temperature, especially the eggs and butter. Preheat the oven 15 minutes before you need it. Assemble utensils: standard measuring cups and spoons, bowls, spatula, wooden spoons, electric mixer and baking pan. Before beginning, fill the kitchen sink with warm soapy water. As you finish with each utensil, place it in the sink. This goes a long way toward keeping a tidy kitchen.

Earthquake Cake

MAKES 10 TO 12 SERVINGS

Topping

2   cups powdered sugar

2   (3-ounce) packages cream
    cheese, softened

1   teaspoon vanilla

Cake

1   cup coconut

1   cup chopped pecans

1   (18-ounce) package German
    Chocolate cake mix

Topping

Cream sugar, cream cheese and vanilla. Set aside.

Cake

Preheat oven to 350 degrees. Grease and flour a 13x9x2 inch baking dish. Combine coconut and pecans. Spread in bottom of dish. Prepare cake mix according to package directions. Pour batter over coconut and nut layer. Do not stir. Drop topping mixture by spoonfuls over cake without coming in contact with sides of dish. Do not stir. Bake 55 minutes or until toothpick or cake tester comes out clean. Cool in pan 5 minutes. Run a knife around edges and invert onto a serving plate. May be served plain or with whipped cream or ice cream.

FRAN'S NOTE

Although it has been more than 14 years since hurricane Hugo hit Charleston on a Thursday evening, I will never forget that we had 4 large wedding receptions scheduled for the following Saturday. Three of the receptions canceled on Friday, but the fourth one had many guests in town from California and the client wanted to proceed with the plans for the reception. We knew, then, that in spite of all the devastation and havoc and in the aftermath of the storm, the show must go on. Unfortunately, the reception site was about 25 miles from our shop and power lines and trees were down along the roadway with debris scattered in every direction. Driving was extremely hazardous. However, with extraordinary precautions, we made it, knowing we had to make the best of a terrible situation, even without electricity and water. We made-do, however, with candles for lighting and gas burners for heating the food. Surprisingly, considering the circumstances, everything went well and the guests invited me to come to California when they had an earthquake. Believe it or not, they had an earthquake that same year. No, I did not get to accept their invitation, but making this cake brings back vivid memories of this reception and the California earthquake of 1989.

May Day Festival

May Day was celebrated at James Simons School in the 1930's when I was in first grade. The festival took place across the street on the grounds of the Enston Homes. The highlight of the festival was the dance around the May pole and the crowning of the Queen. I was chosen to be an attendant to one of the candidates and I wore a long, mint-green dress and carried a fifty-cents bouquet of snap dragons. I felt so special on my first big social event.

~Elizabeth Bullock Godfrey

Triple Chocolate Pound Cake

MAKES 12 SERVINGS

1 (18-ounce) package devil's
  food cake mix with pudding

1 (5.1-ounce) package chocolate
  instant pudding mix

1¼ cups water

½ cup vegetable oil

4 large eggs

3 cups semi-sweet chocolate
  chips, divided

½ cup heavy cream

Pecan halves for garnish

Combine cake mix, pudding mix, water, oil and eggs in a large mixing bowl. Beat 2 minutes at medium speed with an electric mixer. Stir in 2 cups chocolate chips. Pour batter into a greased and floured 10x4 inch Bundt pan. Bake at 350 degrees 50 to 55 minutes. Cool in pan on a wire rack 10 to 15 minutes. Remove from pan and cool completely on a wire rack. Combine remaining 1 cup chocolate chips and cream in a small heavy saucepan. Cook over medium heat, stirring constantly, just until chocolate melts. Cool 15 minutes. Drizzle chocolate glaze over cake. Garnish with pecans. Best to refrigerate 4 hours before serving.

On June 28, 1776, Charleston saw the FIRST decisive American victory of the Revolutionary War. Although greatly outnumbered and with vastly inferior armaments, South Carolina troops under Colonel William Moultrie kept the British fleet from entering the harbor and held off the army trying to invade by land. Their small fort of palmetto logs and sand, located on Sullivan's Island at the mouth of the harbor, withstood the fire of the fleet, the round shot sinking harmlessly into the porous logs and soft sand. The fort was later named for Moultrie, and today is a historic landmark administered by the National Park Service and open to visitors daily.

Sherry Cake

MAKES 12 TO 15 SERVINGS

Cake

½ cup chopped pecans

1 (18-ounce) golden butter cake mix

½ cup pale dry sherry

½ cup water

½ cup vegetable oil

4 eggs

Glaze

1 cup sugar

8 tablespoons butter

¼ cup pale dry sherry

¼ cup water

Cake

Grease and flour a 10x4 inch Bundt pan. Sprinkle nuts on bottom of pan. Combine cake mix, sherry, water, oil and eggs in a mixing bowl. Beat 2 minutes. Pour over nuts in pan. Bake at 350 degrees 50 minutes or until cake tester comes out clean. Pour glaze over cake in pan and let stand 30 minutes.

Glaze

Combine sugar, butter, sherry and water in a saucepan. Bring to boil. Cook, stirring constantly, 2 to 3 minutes.

Crème Caramel

MAKES 12 CUSTARD CUPS

2¼ cups sugar, divided

4   cups milk

7   eggs

1   teaspoon vanilla

Place 1 cup sugar in a small saucepan with a few drops of water. Cook on medium heat until sugar is caramelized. Divide caramel among twelve ½ cup ovenproof custard cups. Place cups into two parchment paper-lined 14x11x3 inch baking pans. Simmer milk over low heat. Combine eggs, 1¼ cups sugar and vanilla in a large bowl. Beat until smooth. Slowly pour warm milk into egg mixture and stir until sugar dissolves. Divide cream mixture among cups. Pour hot water around cups in pan to a depth of 1 inch. Carefully place pans in the oven. Bake at 340 degrees 50 minutes or until the center is set and brown. The consistency should resemble flan. To serve, invert onto individual dessert plates and refrigerate.

Sweet Cherry Cobbler

MAKES 8 SERVINGS

2   cups sugar, divided

1   cup milk

2   teaspoons baking powder

¼   teaspoon salt

1¼ cups all-purpose flour

2½ cups canned sweet pitted cherries, divided

1   tablespoon butter, cut in pieces

2   cups boiling water

Preheat oven to 350 degrees. Combine 1 cup sugar, milk, baking powder, salt, flour and 1 cup cherries in a bowl. Blend well. Pour batter into a greased 13x9x2 inch baking dish. Combine remaining 1 cup sugar, 1½ cups cherries, butter and boiling water. Pour over batter. Bake, uncovered, 1 hour. Serve warm.

Tipsy Bread Pudding

MAKES 6 SERVINGS

Bread Pudding

4-5 slices day-old bread, lightly toasted

1 cup raisins

3 eggs, beaten

½ cup plus 2 tablespoons sugar

⅛ teaspoon salt

3 cups milk, scalded

½ teaspoon cinnamon

Bourbon Sauce

16 tablespoons butter, softened

½ cup honey

¼ cup bourbon

Bread Pudding

Butter bread slices well and cut into strips. Place strips in a 13x9x2 inch buttered baking dish. Layer with raisins. Combine eggs, ½ cup sugar, salt and milk and mix well. Pour egg mixture over bread strips. Let bread strips soak up all the liquid. Combine 2 tablespoons sugar and cinnamon. Sprinkle over bread. Bake at 350 degrees 25 minutes. Serve warm with Bourbon sauce.

Bourbon Sauce

Cream butter and honey. Stir in bourbon. Brush over warm bread pudding before serving. Makes 1¾ cups.

Chocolate Pecan Pie

MAKES 8 SERVINGS

2 (1-ounce) unsweetened chocolate squares

¼ cup coffee

2 tablespoons butter or margarine

4 eggs

1 cup light corn syrup

½ cup sugar

1½ cups chopped pecans

1 (9 inch) pie crust, unbaked

6-8 pecan halves

Combine chocolate and coffee in a medium saucepan. Cook, stirring constantly, over low heat until chocolate melts. Remove from heat. Add butter. Stir until butter melts. Cool. Combine eggs, syrup and sugar. Beat until light and fluffy. Gradually stir chocolate into creamed mixture. Add chopped pecans. Pour filling into crust and top with pecan halves. Bake at 400 degrees 10 minutes. Reduce heat to 300 degrees and bake about 35 minutes longer until set.

Spicy Sweet Potato Pie

MAKES 8 SERVINGS

2 large sweet potatoes, boiled and peeled

4 tablespoons butter, melted

1 cup packed brown sugar

½ teaspoon salt

1 teaspoon cinnamon

¼ teaspoon ground nutmeg

1 teaspoon ground ginger

1¼ cups half-and-half, divided

4 large eggs, beaten

1 (9 inch) pie crust, unbaked

Preheat oven to 350 degrees. Purée potatoes in a blender. Add butter, brown sugar, salt, cinnamon, nutmeg, ginger and ½ cup half-and-half and blend well. Whisk together eggs and ¾ cup half-and-half. Add to potato mixture and blend well. Pour filling into pie crust. Bake 50 to 60 minutes.

Dixie Pecan Pie

MAKES 8 SERVINGS

4   eggs

½   cup sugar

½   cup firmly packed light brown
    sugar

1   cup light corn syrup

1   tablespoon all-purpose flour

1   teaspoon vanilla

¼   teaspoon salt

4   tablespoons butter, melted

2   cups pecans, chopped

1   (9 inch) pie crust, unbaked

Whipping cream (optional)

Preheat oven to 350 degrees. In a medium bowl, beat eggs well. Add sugar, brown sugar, corn syrup, flour, vanilla, and salt. Beat until well combined. Fold in melted butter and pecans. Brush pie crust with egg white wash. Pour filling into crust. Bake about 45 minutes or until filling is set. Cool completely on wire rack. Prior to serving, decorate pie with whipped cream.

Yum-Yum Brownies

MAKES APPROXIMATELY 20 BROWNIES

8   tablespoons butter

1   cup sugar

2   eggs, beaten

¾   cup sifted all-purpose flour

¼   teaspoon salt

½   teaspoon baking powder

2   (1-ounce) semi-sweet chocolate
    squares, melted

1   cup nuts

1   teaspoon vanilla

Cream butter and sugar. Add eggs. Sift together flour, salt and baking powder. Stir in dry ingredients. Add chocolate, nuts and vanilla. Pour batter into a greased 8x8x2 inch baking dish. Bake at 350 degrees about 20 minutes.

Coconut Pies

MAKES 16 SERVINGS

1½ cups sugar	8 tablespoons butter
8 eggs	2 cups coconut
4 cups milk	2 (9 inch) pie crusts, unbaked

Beat sugar and eggs about 2 minutes. Warm milk and butter in a saucepan over low heat. Do not boil. Stir in sugar mixture and coconut until well blended. Pour filling into two 9 inch crusts. Bake at 400 degrees 25 to 30 minutes.

FRAN'S NOTE

When an unbaked pie crust is to be filled with a very moist filling, it is best to brush its surface first with a small amount of lightly beaten egg white and then chill the crust. This precaution will prevent the moisture of the filling from penetrating into the lower crust.

Butterscotch Squares

MAKES 36 SQUARES

8 tablespoons margarine	3 eggs
1 (16-ounce) box light brown sugar	2 cups self-rising flour
	1½ cups chopped pecans

Combine margarine and brown sugar in top of double boiler. Cook until sugar is melted. Set aside and cool. Add eggs, one at a time, beating well after each addition. Beat in flour and add nuts. Pour batter into a 12x8x2 inch baking dish. Bake at 350 degrees about 30 minutes.

Mom's Custard Pie

MAKES 6 TO 8 SERVINGS

1 (9 inch) pie crust, unbaked	1 teaspoon vanilla
4 eggs	2½ cups milk
½ cup sugar	¼ teaspoon ground nutmeg
¼ teaspoon salt	

Line an unpierced pie crust with a double thickness of heavy-duty foil. Bake at 450 degrees 8 minutes. Remove foil and bake 5 minutes longer. Remove from the oven and set aside. Separate one egg and set the white aside. In a mixing bowl, beat the yolk and remaining eggs just until combined. Blend in sugar, salt and vanilla. Stir in milk. Beat reserved egg white until stiff peaks form. Fold into custard. Carefully pour custard into crust. Cover pie edges with foil. Bake 15 to 20 minutes or until a knife inserted near the center comes out clean. Cool on a wire rack. Sprinkle with nutmeg. Store in the refrigerator.

Over-Sized Chocolate Chip Cookies

MAKES 60 COOKIES

32 tablespoons butter, softened (4 sticks)	4½ cups all-purpose flour
1½ cups sugar	2 teaspoons baking soda
1½ cups packed brown sugar	1 teaspoon salt
2 teaspoons vanilla	4 cups semi-sweet chocolate chips
4 eggs	2 cups chopped pecans

Cream butter, sugar, brown sugar and vanilla. Add eggs, one at a time, beating well after each addition. Gradually beat in flour, baking soda and salt. Stir in chocolate chips and pecans. Drop dough by rounded tablespoonfuls 2 inches apart onto an ungreased baking sheet. Bake at 350 degrees 10 to 12 minutes or until lightly brown.

Carolina Tarts

MAKES 24 TARTS

Cream Cheese Pastry

8	tablespoons butter, softened	1	cup all-purpose flour
1	(3-ounce) package cream cheese, softened		

Filling

8	tablespoons butter, softened	¾	cup raisins, chopped
1	cup sugar	1	cup pecans, chopped
2	eggs, separated	2	teaspoons vanilla

Cream Cheese Pastry

Cream butter and cream cheese. Add flour and mix until smooth. Cover and refrigerate. Turn out dough onto floured surface. Roll to ¼ inch thickness. Cut dough with 1½ inch biscuit cutter. Line greased miniature muffin cups with dough.

Filling

Cream butter and sugar. Blend in egg yolks. Beat egg whites with a fork until foamy. Add to creamed butter mixture. Add raisins, nuts and vanilla. Spoon filling into pastry lined muffin cups. Bake at 325 degrees 20 to 25 minutes or until filling is set.

Almond Bites

MAKES ABOUT 40

8 tablespoons butter, softened

1 cup sugar

1 cup ground almonds

1 egg, beaten

½ teaspoon almond extract

¾ cup all-purpose flour

1 teaspoon baking powder

1 teaspoon raspberry jam (optional)

⅓ cup finely chopped, blanched almonds

Preheat oven to 375 degrees. Cream butter and sugar until smooth. Add ground almonds, egg and almond extract. Sift together flour and baking powder. Add dry ingredients and mix to a soft dough. Drop dough by rounded teaspoonfuls 2 inches apart onto parchment paper-lined baking sheet. Spoon a small amount of jam in the center. Sprinkle with chopped almonds. Bake 10 minutes. Cool completely on wire rack.

Heath Bars

MAKES 48 BARS

16 tablespoons butter, softened

½ cup packed brown sugar

½ cup sugar

1 egg yolk

1 teaspoon vanilla

1 cup self-rising flour

1½ cups semi-sweet chocolate chips, melted

½ cup slivered almonds

Cream butter, brown sugar and sugar. Add egg yolk and vanilla. Stir in flour until well blended. Press mixture into a 15x10x1 inch jelly-roll pan. Bake at 325 degrees 20 minutes or until edges are lightly brown. Remove from oven. Spread melted chocolate over baked layer. Sprinkle with almonds. Cut into squares while still warm.

Cherry Coconut Bars

MAKES 15 TO 20 SERVINGS

1¼ cups all-purpose flour, divided

8 tablespoons butter, softened

3 tablespoons powdered sugar

1 cup sugar

2 eggs

1 teaspoon vanilla

1 cup chopped pecans

¾ cup fresh or frozen coconut

¾ cup maraschino cherries, drained and chopped

Mix together 1 cup flour, butter and powdered sugar. Press mixture into a 13x9x2 inch baking pan. Bake at 350 degrees 25 minutes. In the meantime, combine sugar and eggs. Stir in ¼ cup flour, vanilla, pecans, coconut and cherries. Spread filling over baked crust. Bake at 350 degrees 25 minutes. Cool and cut into bite-size bars.

FRAN'S NOTE

When baking, add extracts or flavoring to the
shortening during the creaming process to minimize evaporation.
A rule of thumb is to use 1 teaspoon of the extract or flavoring per
pint of food, unless the flavoring is extra strength.

Strawberry-Raspberry Parfait

MAKES 6 TO 8 SERVINGS

1 (10-ounce) package frozen raspberries, thawed	2 cups strawberries, sliced
½ cup sugar	2 teaspoons lemon juice
2 tablespoons cornstarch	1 quart vanilla ice cream
	1 cup sour cream

Drain raspberries, reserving syrup. Add enough water to syrup to make 1 cup liquid. In a small saucepan, combine sugar and cornstarch. Stir in raspberry syrup. Add strawberries. Cook and stir over medium-high heat until mixture boils and thickens. Remove from heat and stir in raspberries and lemon juice. Refrigerate sauce. In parfait glasses, layer ice cream, berry sauce, sour cream, then more sauce. Repeat layers. Top with a scoop of ice cream.

Cinnamon Crisps

MAKES APPROXIMATELY 60 CRISPS

16 tablespoons margarine, softened	2 cups all-purpose flour
1 cup sugar	2 teaspoons cinnamon
1 egg, separated	½ teaspoon salt
	1 cup pecans, chopped

Preheat oven to 275 degrees. Cream margarine and sugar. Blend in egg yolk. In a separate bowl, combine flour, cinnamon and salt. Add dry ingredients to creamed mixture. Press mixture onto a greased 15x10x1 inch jelly-roll pan. Pat down with dampened hands. Beat egg white with a fork. Brush over dough layer. Sprinkle with nuts and brush again with egg white wash. Bake 45 minutes. Cut into 1x2 inch rectangles while hot.

Rachel's Favorite Pumpkin Cake Roll

MAKES 15 SERVINGS

Cake

¼ cup powdered sugar

¾ cup all-purpose flour

½ teaspoon baking powder

½ teaspoon baking soda

1 teaspoon cinnamon

½ teaspoon ground cloves

¼ teaspoon salt

3 eggs

1 cup sugar

⅔ cup canned pumpkin

1 cup nuts, chopped

Filling

1 (8-ounce) package cream
  cheese, softened

1 cup powdered sugar

6 tablespoons butter, softened

1 teaspoon vanilla

Powdered sugar

Line a 15x10 inch jelly-roll pan with wax paper. Grease and flour paper. Sprinkle towel with powdered sugar. Combine flour, baking powder, baking soda, cinnamon, cloves and salt in small bowl. In a separate large bowl, beat eggs and sugar until thick. Beat in pumpkin. Stir in flour mixture and nuts. Spread evenly onto prepared pan. Bake at 400 degrees 10 to 12 minutes or till cake top springs back when touched. Immediately loosen and invert cake onto prepared towel. Carefully peel off paper. Roll up cake with towel starting with narrow end. Cool cake roll on wire rack. Beat cream cheese, powdered sugar, butter and vanilla. Carefully unroll cake, gently removing the towel. Spread cream cheese filling over cake. Reroll cake. Wrap in plastic and refrigerate 2 hours. Sprinkle with powdered sugar before serving.

Megan's Mini Cheese Cakes

MAKES 24 MINI CAKES

Cake

½ cup sugar

1 (8-ounce) package cream cheese, softened

2 eggs

¾ teaspoon vanilla

Topping

1 cup sour cream

¼ cup sugar

¾ teaspoon vanilla

Cream sugar and cream cheese until smooth. Add eggs and vanilla and mix well. Divide batter among 24 paper-lined miniature muffin cups. Bake at 325 degrees 15 minutes. Meanwhile, combine sour cream, sugar and vanilla for topping. Remove cakes from oven and add a small teaspoonful of topping. Return to oven and bake 5 minutes longer. Cool. May be garnished with fruit.

FRAN'S NOTE

Megan, our granddaughter, is one of our greatest fans, especially when it comes to the mini cheese cakes. She never leaves the shop without checking the refrigerator to see if there are any cheese cakes with her name written on them.

INDEX

Q

R

Catering to Charleston

HAMBY CATERING
925 ST. ANDREWS BLVD.
CHARLESTON, SC 29407
PHONE: 843-571-3103 FAX: 843-556-8396
EMAIL: HAMBYCOOKBOOK@BELLSOUTH.NET
TO ORDER ONLINE, VISIT OUR WEB PAGE: WWW.CATERINGTOCHARLESTON.COM

NAME _____

ADDRESS _____

CITY _____ STATE _____

ZIP _____ PHONE _____

PLEASE SEND _____ COPIES OF *Catering to Charleston* @ $22.95 EACH _____

SC RESIDENTS ONLY ADD 6% SALES TAX @ $ 1.38 EACH _____

SHIPPING AND HANDLING @ $ 4.50 EACH _____

TOTAL ENCLOSED _____

MAKE CHECK PAYABLE TO: *Catering to Charleston*.

PLEASE CHARGE TO: VISA / MASTERCARD (CIRCLE ONE) CARD NUMBER: _____

EXPIRATION DATE: _____ SIGNATURE: _____

- -

Catering to Charleston

HAMBY CATERING
925 ST. ANDREWS BLVD.
CHARLESTON, SC 29407
PHONE: 843-571-3103 FAX: 843-556-8396
EMAIL: HAMBYCOOKBOOK@BELLSOUTH.NET
TO ORDER ONLINE, VISIT OUR WEB PAGE: WWW.CATERINGTOCHARLESTON.COM

NAME _____

ADDRESS _____

CITY _____ STATE _____

ZIP _____ PHONE _____

PLEASE SEND _____ COPIES OF *Catering to Charleston* @ $22.95 EACH _____

SC RESIDENTS ONLY ADD 6% SALES TAX @ $ 1.38 EACH _____

SHIPPING AND HANDLING @ $ 4.50 EACH _____

TOTAL ENCLOSED _____

MAKE CHECK PAYABLE TO: *Catering to Charleston*.

PLEASE CHARGE TO: VISA / MASTERCARD (CIRCLE ONE) CARD NUMBER: _____

EXPIRATION DATE: _____ SIGNATURE: _____

Greek Garlic Chicken

¼ cup olive oil   2 tsps lemon juice

1 tsp garlic powder

cook chicken in this or   brush on baked chick

White Bean Salad

15 oz can cannellini or great Northern rinsed & drain

2 TBLS olive oil   ½ tsp dried basil

2 tsps rice vinegar   ¼ tsp garlic powder

1 tsp lemon juice   ⅛ tsp sugar

warm or cold

Spinach dip

15 oz can spinach well drained   ¼ tsp garlic powder

1 cup plain yogurt   "   onion powder

½ cup mayonnaise   ⅛ tsp salt

                     tsp of lemon juice to taste

Tomato - Corn Relish

14.5 oz can diced tomatoes, drain

15 oz can corn   drained

4 oz can diced grchles, drained

3 TBLS olive oil   2 TBLS rice vinegar   ⅛ tsp onion powd

seal in airtight jar

Crustless Cheese Tart   325° oven

                          greased cake pan
                                tart pan

12 oz evaporated milk

heat milk + ¼ cup of water

add cheese ¼ tsp onion powder   pinch cayenne

            ¼ tsp salt

beat 3 eggs   Bake for 40 minutes